# LIFE AFTER DEAF

The inspiring true story of one woman's fight to
overcome a mysterious illness and redefine her life

# Monique Williamson

Prominence Publishing. www.prominencepublishing.com

Publisher's Note: Although the author and publisher have made every effort to ensure that the information in this book was correct at press time, the author and publisher do not assume and hereby disclaim any liability to any party for any loss, damage, or disruption caused by errors or omissions, whether such errors or omissions result from negligence, accident, or any other cause.

This book is not intended as a substitute for the medical advice of physicians. The reader should regularly consult a physician in matters relating to his/her health and particularly with respect to any symptoms that may require diagnosis or medical attention.

The views expressed herein belong entirely to the author and are not necessarily those of the publisher.

Life After Deaf / Monique Williamson. -- 1st ed.

ISBN 978-1-988925-39-4

# Dedication

This book is dedicated to my husband Jesse, who stood by my side through dozens of unexpected traumas, and chose to marry me, even though I was a deaf woman who might never hear the sound of his voice again. His commitment to my soul and his undying love for me can never be understated.

To my mum Romy and my stepfather David, who were always by my side, and by the sides of my husband and children when they needed help with care and food preparation while I was absent from their lives.

To my firstborn daughter Rachael, the moment I laid eyes on her I felt a newfound sense of inner strength to make much needed changes in my life. Years later she always held my hand during my many hospital stays telling me that I would be ok; she just knew it inside. I am thankful for her bravery during a time when I was unable to hear her voice or comfort her when she may have needed it, because I was too sick in the hospital.

To my infant son Jack, for being a happy baby who slept through the night after only a few months, and who adjusted instantly to formula bottles when strong medications negated my ability to nurse him.

To my father Michael who, whenever in my life the chips were down, always bailed me out. He generously bought me a new computer to ensure my story could be shared with the world.

To Dr. Michael Smith ENT, Dr. Shahin Nabi ENT and Dr. Kevin McLeod, Internal Medicine. These three doctors have angel wings and are not to be considered average by any means. On any given day, at any given hour, these men would drop anything to ensure my care and comfort. They are a part of my story and shall always remain a part of my pain and my journey into healing.

To Dr. Greg Monkewich, who changed my life and ended my suffering after 5 long years when he finally put a name to my illness and started me on life saving medications.

To Dr. Jane Lea and Dr. Westerberg of St. Paul's ENT department. They gave me the gift of the Cochlear implant, and the miracle of sound once again.

To Heather Southam, Audiologist; a kind and patient woman who would also drop anything at any time to see me.

To the doctors and nurses in the ER at Lionsgate hospital who were patient and kind to me on multiple visits over three agonizing and painful years. Your kind care will never be forgotten.

Finally, this book is dedicated to all the friends in my life who have shared their miracles with me, and have taken the time to allow me to share mine. Your text messages and social media comments that offered encouragement and words of support were an integral part of my mental survival throughout my many battles.

My hope in sharing my story is that I can reach the men and women who suffer what seem like insurmountable battles in their lives. Whether physically disabled, suffering from chronic pain, addiction, mental illness, sudden tragedy, or any situation that brings them into a seemingly endless abyss of pain and affliction, you are not alone.

This is the story of my journey through darkness, and the tools I used to find my way.

Blessings,
Monique

# Table of Contents

# CHAPTER ONE

# Sudden Deafness

It felt like I was in the middle of a nightmare, only this time I knew it was real, and I wasn't going to wake up. I was stretched out on a gurney, crammed up against a wall in an overcrowded and bustling Emergency Room. The day was unseasonably hot for April in Vancouver, and it added to my level of discomfort as I lay in a pool of my own sweat.

The shortage of nurses and exceptionally long wait times only served to prolong my personal hell and misery. I was going deaf and the last remaining natural sounds I would ever hear were fading away with each passing minute. All I could do was helplessly observe as my world as I had known it began to unravel.

My gaze was fixated on a speaker in the ceiling directly above me. I could still hear sounds, but oddly that's all they were. No sense could be made as my brain struggled to recognize what was now just noise. It was a bizarre sensation to know that those speakers were delivering messages that everyone around me could hear, but that I could no longer make sense of; it was beyond unsettling. It was like my brain was reaching and striving to no avail. On top of that din, inside my head I could hear what sounded like a pair of runners clunking around in a dryer.

Boom-boom, boom-boom.

As I listened to the loud internal thudding and the noise from the speakers, I became aware that I was alone within my body, and I feared there would be no way to accurately convey to anyone exactly what I was experiencing. I realized that even the best machines or the most skilled doctors would not be able to comprehend what I was hearing. I began to panic, thinking, *'What if this is it? What if this boom-boom, boom-boom inside my head is what I must listen to for the rest of my life?* That whirring and thumping, like runners in a dryer, was unbearable, but if no one could hear it but me, then how could they ever help me?

I had just been to visit the ENT hours earlier and explained that when Jesse and Rachael came home and spoke to me, they sounded like Alvin and the Chipmunks, as if they had just inhaled helium. I asked them why they were talking like that, and when they looked at each other confused, I realized they were not joking, and panic rushed over me.

Within minutes of my arrival, I was in the sound booth being tested, and the news was dire. **It was going; the only remaining hearing I had.** My left ear was already gone; it had been for the past eight months (sudden deafness), and despite my ENT promising me that lightning never strikes twice… it did for me. He handed me a piece of paper and told me to hurry and get myself to the ER across the street. He said I would be admitted to the hospital and that he would be there shortly to oversee my care. I had 30 percent hearing left, and apparently that's not enough; at least not in the decibel range where I had lost it. In order to hear voices and make out what people are saying, I needed more frequency and range. It was as if voices were just beyond my reach.

The doctors ran around me as I lay on my stretcher. The time I had alone to think about what was happening to me was torturous. When my husband arrived by my side, I instantly mourned the loss of hearing his voice as he mouthed the words "I love you" and "You'll be ok".

I knew I would never hear him again, and there are no words to describe that feeling. All I could think was, 'What will my life be like? Will I hear this rumbling in my head forever? Is this what happens when you go deaf, you hear sounds in your head?' I would rather hear nothing at all, as this would surely make a person go insane.

# There are no accidents.

Throughout my life, whenever I needed help or wanted to achieve something specific, I set the intention and visualized my desired outcome and somehow, some way, I found myself living that intention. I always felt like I was guided and that if I wasn't sure which way to turn, a tiny voice in my head would lead the way. I call it my intuition or inner guidance system.

Another thing I noticed, maybe because I was open to it, is that the guidance always seemed purposeful and <u>specific</u>. If I asked for it, I would get it, and sometimes I found I needed to be careful what I wished for. In fact, many times the things I asked for seemed **crappy** at the moment I received them, but looking back, I could always see why things unfolded as they did.

I remember when I had my first child, Rachael, and she was only a year old. I was desperately unhappy in my personal life. I wanted to end my marriage of twelve years. The relationship was no longer serving either my ex-husband or I, but for some reason I felt totally paralyzed to make a needed change.

When our daughter was born, it was no longer about just me and my needs and wants. The importance of her being surrounded by two happy parents, whether it meant being together or separating, became the focus. It was her precious life, and she needed to be raised in a peaceful environment. Despite knowing that separation was the best decision, I found myself unable to find the courage to take the leap. My mind chattered away negatively, telling myself that alone I'd surely fail, and I'd likely have no way to support myself.

I was an insecure woman, and always had been since the day my dad suddenly left my mom for another woman when I was eight years old. Since that time, I've always had the notion that I was not worthy of love. I associated his leaving with abandonment, which translated in my subconscious mind that somehow,

I needed a man to fill a void. I worried about how I would make ends meet now that I had the greater responsibility of a child to help care for.

I had been a top producing sales executive in every company that I had ever worked for, so why did I doubt my ability?

I was out of shape, felt frumpy, and had just cut off all my hair into a post-baby mommy cut. I lacked confidence through and through. I had also left all my high school mates behind over the years and had amassed a large group of new friends, but they were all in my husband's circle, too. They were "couple friends." If we were to split our friends would have to be told that we were not happy after a baby and thirteen years together. I would feel ashamed, embarrassed and judged, as well as being worried that they might all choose to be his friend and not mine. We owned two homes and had started a pizza franchise. All of it would have to be sold...it was a lot to handle. It seemed as insurmountable as climbing Everest at the time.

So, feeling extremely defeated and hopeless, I curled up in a fetal position on my bed and just cried. I cried, and cried, and cried some more, until there were no more tears. Then I began to pray out loud to God and asked him to kindly help me. I said, "Please, if you can hear me, can you just show me a sign that you are here and that you can hear me?"

I'll never forget the weather that day. The sky was dark grey and covered with thick clouds. It only served to add more gloom to my already dark mood. As I lay talking, as if by magic, my room slowly began to light up from one corner to the other, as if a cloud blew aside and allowed the sun to peer through. The room lit slowly, and then just as I was becoming aware of what was happening, the room was once again grey. I stood up and looked out the window, but there was no sun, and no possibility of the heavy obscured skies having allowed it through.

*'Ok, you're listening.'* I thought. As goosebumps covered my body, I decided to ask another question. What did I have to lose? *'What job should I pursue so I can be a mom to my baby and still get my own home and pay my mortgage?'* I did not want to live in a condo because I was sure I wanted a yard for my daughter and dog to play in. I also needed a good income that would allow enough freedom and flexibility for me to still be a parent. Soon after I made my request, a voice as clear and loud as you can imagine spoke to me, but this was no ordinary voice. The voice was in my head and it said two words, "REAL ESTATE." I was stunned, of course, as this voice was not beside me or in another room but in my head, and it was not my mind chatter. This was a different kind of voice; one that I had never heard before. It was loud and deep, and it echoed. I can still hear it now when I think about it. It was a day I will never forget, and it was guidance that no one on earth can tell me doesn't exist. That experience shook me to the core. *If you ask, and you believe, you shall receive.*

I ran to my kitchen and fumbled about with the cordless phone. I was frantically pressing buttons trying to reach my dad, which seemed to take an eternity. When he answered, I was so full of enthusiasm that I could barely get the words out. "Dad, Dad, listen," as if he had a choice, "I know what sales job I should do where I'll be able to make enough money to afford my mortgage payments and still have free time to spend with Rachael." I asked him to please lend me the money to buy a laptop and help me pay for the real estate course, so I could start right way. I told him I had a plan, and I needed to do it.

Within three months I had passed the real estate exam, which was no easy feat considering I was up six times a night nursing a sleepless baby and the fact that it had a 70 percent fail rate. I was working within four months, selling homes with a local real estate team. In a very short time, I could already see my ability sprouting beyond my current outfit and I branched out on my own. After three years I became the top selling realtor in my office. I was asked to speak at and host lunch-and-learn sessions, where some of the top agents in the industry came to hear me! I will never forget some of the real estate legends that showed up; it was surreal. Some of them had been selling for more than twenty years! I knew then that I was exactly where I was supposed to be.

Around that same time that I passed my real estate exam, I finally worked up the courage to split up with my husband. The painful process of estimating the value of our assets began, and I started looking for somewhere to live. I was determined to buy myself a small house in the same area I was in. In order for things to work with the new purchase, I needed to ensure it had a few specific requirements: namely a suite that I could rent to a tenant to help with the mortgage payments.

I learned how to search for homes on the MLS with my new job, and every day I would check for new listings hoping a match would show up for me, but nothing ever seemed to make the checklist, at least not in my budget.

I was very specific when I entered my search criteria. I determined that it must have two kitchens, so a mortgage helper was imperative, yet for some reason, this one-level rancher with no second kitchen kept coming up on my screen. It was $130,000 over my budget with no revenue suite. I looked at the pictures once and thought, 'Wow!' It was a West Coast style home with twelve-foot high ceilings and lovely cedar beams. It had skylights, a wood-burning fireplace, a huge private stone patio in the back; perfect for a child to ride a trike, and a lawn as well. The kitchen had a large centre island that overlooked a cozy family room, too. It was perfect, but it was way too much money! For the next few days I kept searching, and each day the same house found its way onto my screen.

One day I was in tears, just having a hard time dealing with my life, so I put the baby in the car and went for a drive. The area

I lived in was nice, but it was in a mountain shadow and it felt dark that day. *'I have to get out of here,'* I thought to myself as I drove up over the hill and into the sunshine. I had no idea it was even sunny that day, and then it struck me that I wanted to live in a brighter place. I kept driving, with no destination in mind, just to get away from the house and clear my head, enjoying the sunshine. As my car went down the other side of the hill, I saw an open house sign. I thought to myself how strange it was being a Tuesday morning, as I thought open houses were only on weekends.

I decided to follow the signs to see it. I had no idea where I was, but after following seven arrows, taking four rights and three lefts, I ended up in front of my destination. I sat out in front for a moment and assessed the home. The driveway looked so familiar. That's when it dawned on me. *'Oh my goodness!'* I realized I was sitting in front of the '$130,000 over my budget, no revenue suite, one-level dream home' that kept appearing on my screen. What are the odds?

I went inside and it seemed as if everything was set up especially for my daughter and me. The place reminded me of the home I grew up in. It had the same cedar beams and beautiful high peaked ceilings. Natural light poured in through the skylights, and from the front door I could smell the wood log burning in the fireplace. The house was located in a sought-after village in one of the safest neighbourhoods, and I remember saying to myself, *'If I can move here, then I can do this. I can live here happy and alone, and I would feel safe doing it.'*

I called my dad again, unable to string my enthusiastic sentences together. I pleaded with him to believe me when I said that I had found the house. I knew when I got there, and the way I got there, and by the fact that it was that same pesky house that kept appearing on my computer; despite not meeting my criteria, that it was the home meant for me. I was led there somehow, and I knew I had to find a way to buy it.

I asked him to lend me the difference, short term, just until I got my business running. Dad had seen me sell and he trusted in my ability. He wanted to see his granddaughter end up in the right home, even if it meant him helping us in the interim.

That night I made an offer on the house, and the owner, a paraplegic man named Gary, decided he wanted his home to go to my daughter and me. He accepted our offer before the first public open houses even happened, because he wanted his beloved home to go to a family that would love it and enjoy it as much as he had. He could have waited for all the people to show up on the weekend and perhaps generate more bids, but he heard my story and he knew I loved his home. The possibility of making a few thousand more dollars was not important to him. The home was ours! I couldn't help but feel that something had guided us there, and that was no accident.

These mini miracles keep occurring in my life, and they seem so purposeful. The result has really changed the way I perceive things. I feel less alone and have a far greater sense of inner peace and purpose. During my darkest hours, when I feel like I am about to face the impossible, suddenly my troubles seem surmountable, and I became unstoppable. The shift in my thinking from "I'm alone," or "I can't," and, "It's not possible," transform to "I can," "I will," and "I'm never alone."

My seemingly unhappy life became happier and I was armed with my new sense of purpose; I attracted like-minded people who helped me achieve things I never dreamed were possible. Our new home became our strengthening sanctuary. It was a haven for my soul to experience exponential and much-needed growth which would take me into the next chapter of my life.

The next ten years of my life were a spiritual roller coaster. I tried to find my way as a single mother, juggling an infant and a career. There was a huge part of me that still felt lonely at times, so I also tried to navigate the dating scene.

Dating when I was in my thirties was a whole lot different than when I was in my twenties. To begin with, there was no such thing as 'online dating' when I was in my early twenties. You met people out and about in the world... not online. I just wanted to meet a nice man but resisted creating any kind of profile as it just didn't feel right to me initially. I was still in a big growth phase of my life, having just ended a thirteen-year union. I felt it was important to reflect on what mistakes I may have made there, so history would not repeat itself. I was also trying to regain confidence, create new friendships, and navigate my new job. It was chaos, frankly. You learn very quickly when you're not whole yet, that finding and attracting the right relationship is just not possible.

Any romance I found was just infatuation; I would feel a momentary high that was superficial. It fed my ego and silenced the negative mind chatter for a short time. If your mind is allowed to run rampant and unchecked, it will tell you *"you've failed! you're not worthy, you're no longer attractive post-baby, no one will want you now that you have a child..."* so on, and so forth. So, when you have a man in front of you that you actually feel attracted to and he tells you everything you think you want to hear, you get a high. It's kind of like a drug addiction.

I've always held the belief that we emit a certain vibration, like an energy frequency. If we feel happy, we emit higher vibrations than if we feel depressed. I found that when I was very happy and I thought positively, I would attract more of the same. Similarly, if I was thinking negative thoughts, I would attract more negative things.

My addiction to the brief high I would get from a man telling me I was beautiful was dangerous, because I was in a growth phase in my life and didn't feel whole, so the vibration I was emitting was all over the map. Sadly, that meant so too were the men I was attracting. This was good and bad. The good news, looking back, was that at each level I reached on my journey to find wholeness, I met someone who mirrored my own issues right back to me. In other words, they too had issues to work through, and usually similar ones to mine. It forced me to look deeper within myself and then change my behaviour, ultimately moving on to the next person because it wasn't working.

I enjoyed the thrill of discovery—but hated the reality checks. What followed was a morbid nine years that were filled with so many emotions. I wished I could find Mr. Right, and fast. The problem was that the Mr. Right I always envisioned, and told all my friends about, was a tall order. Similar to creating that 'online dating' wish list that would turn over few results. There was a list a mile long. The man I dreamt about would need to be spiritually evolved, patient, kind, charismatic, independent, enjoy fitness but not yoga, be attractive, and he must love kids! Easy, right? That's what I told my friends I wanted at age thirty-one. I described him, my fairytale wedding, the baby we would have, and even the baby's name: Jack. I had so many details that even to this day, my friends remind me of how perfectly I manifested my current situation.

As a young child, all I wanted was to have a true love. Everyone has a different destiny in their life, but I felt strongly that mine was to meet my Prince Charming and live happily ever after. I didn't realize I was so broken emotionally, and how much heartache that would cause me along the way.

I was so frustrated with life at age thirty-nine. I was successful in business, a good mother, an avid fitness buff, had an active social life, and yet I was unbalanced spiritually. In order to live my best life, I figured that I needed to devote equal amounts of time to all the sectors of my life. Those sectors were family, work, fitness, health, and spirituality.

There was far too much imbalance. I wasn't taking proper care of my health; both physically and mentally. I wasn't taking time each day to just allow myself the space to feel gratitude, nor was I staying present in the moment. I always wanted to improve something or look ahead to my future, and as a result I failed to see how much beauty and love I already had. I was so blessed by anyone else's standard, but my mind was in control of my thoughts, and it wasn't satisfied. I allowed the internal tapes to play and tell me I wasn't good enough, that I needed a relationship to define me, and more material items to fill the voids. Somehow, I thought that the more that I achieved, the better I'd be.

This slippery slope I was on is much too common in this three-dimensional world we believe to be our be-all and end-all. The world we are born into is built on consumerism where we define ourselves by material goods, social status, and how we look. Magazines aren't written about the power of living in the moment, or how beauty is more than skin deep; they are written about how to lose ten pounds in six days, or how to apply contour makeup to hide your imperfect face.

Everywhere I looked reminded me I was not meeting the criteria of our society, so it was no wonder that I felt broken and depressed. Worse still was my relentlessly negative mind chatter. My mind caused me great stress, and it was not until I learned to ignore its commentary and replace it with positive affirmations that I started to see a real light at the end of my tunnel.

Trying to work with the chatter was my best bet, because I knew it wouldn't stop. It's part of the human experience. It's your ego-mind, and it only exists in our earthly body, and not in our soul. Working with this chatter is like working out because it takes constant training. You train with weights, you build muscle, you get stronger. It's the same thing when it comes to changing your thoughts about yourself. Your self-talk can be trained exactly like a muscle. Repetitions. When I learned to silence the negativity and train myself to accept that my life perfect as it was (with or without Mr. Right) everything fel place. I realized that I *was* good enough, but it was one thing to say it to myself; I needed to prove it and break all of the bad habits that accompanied my seeming unworthiness.

Actions speak louder than words, and for me to succeed, I knew I needed to exercise some follow-through. Old relationships that were built from the negative mind chatter needed to be terminated—primarily because they were built on a version of myself that I no longer wanted. I preferred to shed that skin. The doors I closed were quickly followed with new ones that opened wide into a world unknown to me previously. This world I was about to enter was the world I dreamt of as a small child. It was a world filled with magic, a prince, and maybe even a real-life fairytale.

# CHAPTER TWO

# The Fairytale

I'll never forget 2013. It was a year filled with so much emotional turmoil.

I wanted to achieve more in my business, get rid of a bunch of fake friends, and I really wanted it to be the year that a guy I had liked for the past three years and I could finally be together (despite knowing better!). In order to protect his identity, I will refer to him going forward, as Tom. Tom and I had met randomly through friends at a pub. We kept in contact and seemed to keep crossing paths for the next few years. He was successful and handsome, had his own home, and for some reason I visualized him as being the guy I had waited for my whole life.

There was only one small problem; Tom had a girlfriend that he was on and off with. Stupidly, I became his sympathetic ear. I thought I was being smart by being a friend to him and allowing him to lean on me and by offering him support. I waited patiently on the sidelines while he assured me he was trying to end things with her. I even went so far as to think of him as noble because he was trying to do it in a nice way and not hurt her feelings. How stupid could I be? I actually thought my patience would result in the two of us having a dream relationship.

He was unavailable, and I guess so was I, because I attracted him into my life repeatedly. He would see me when times with his girlfriend were supposedly dire and over. He was done, *or so he would say*. He would come and confide in me and make me feel special because I was his confidant; I was the one he trusted enough to tell about his shitty relationship. Perhaps I was engaged by him because he was seemingly unreachable. It was always the same old story, "I like you, but I just need more time to deal with 'my situation.'" 'The situation' took three years to deal with, and never got officially dealt with until October of 2013.

Over the summer, he and I had had our most intimate times, texting one another from afar. He was five hours away by car. I felt sure that when he returned in the fall that we would finally be together, and all my patience would be worth it! He told me it was over with her, and that he had moved away for the summer to get away from her to ensure that it was finally the end.

Of course, I was being stupid, but I was not stupid enough, thankfully, to leave all my eggs in his basket. Even so, my mind longed for the eventual "us." I was still dating other men who were equally unavailable, hoping I would find my happily ever after. For some reason, however, Tom stuck in my mind as the one I secretly wanted to cast as the Prince in my fairytale.

It was the Fall of 2013. I saw on Facebook that he was back in Vancouver and had not contacted me yet. I was pissed off to say the least. Never one to hold back my emotions, I sent him a two-hundred-word private message telling him, in no uncertain terms, what I thought of him and his bullshit.

That night I had plans with another guy; a hilarious friend that I had met while at the company golf tournament. It was in late September every year that our real estate office hosted the annual company golf tournament. I signed up every year, even though I am not the greatest golfer. I love the comradery and the networking that takes place at these amazing events.

I was placed in a foursome with my great friend Leah, and two men: Jesse and Steve. From the moment I got there, I was in tears with laughter as our foursome navigated the course with the rest of our office. It was music, beer, a few photos, and just a really great time.

I had met Jesse a year earlier at the company Christmas party. He was the son of a woman that worked in my office that I had befriended years ago – a highly successful agent who I used to visit on occasion when I needed some business advice. Jesse was just a few inches taller than me. He was very handsome, and to call him charming was an understatement. He had lighter sandy-colored hair, and piercing, bright brown squinty eyes that seemed almost backlit. His personality was electric. His sense of humour was what drew me, and anyone who knows him, in. He was intelligent, warm, kind, and considerate of others. He was also twenty-five years old, and I was thirty-nine, so I was not thinking of Jesse as a possible date. I was simply enjoying the company of my foursome that day, and not thinking about anyone else.

After the tournament, Jesse sat across from me and told me I should get on the bus with him and ride back to the office. I already had a ride, so I declined.

I never forgot that afternoon though for some reason. He made me laugh so much, and I really enjoyed the dynamic of the group. I wanted to recreate that day and reached out to all of them and suggested we have a get-together. Steve and Leah were always busy, and somehow Jesse and I decided that he would come over and we would have a few drinks and a laugh. I had no intention or even a thought in my mind that I wanted anything with him besides friendship. I just wanted to drink wine and be carefree and laugh, and Jesse was just the guy to do that with.

He came over and I thought it might be awkward, as it was just he and I, but from the first moment our conversation was easy; like we had been friends for years. We sat in my "chill lounge" (as I liked to refer to my living room) from 6:00 until 10:00, and the time flew by. Hours seemed like minutes, and I think we polished off several bottles of wine in the process. We talked about everything. Jesse shared a lot of his personal goals and values and how he believed strongly in the power of our thoughts and the importance of keeping them in check. He was at a crossroads in his life, as I was, and I comfortably shared with him all my personal struggles, and even my dreams of ditching good old Tom.

Jesse was fourteen years younger than me, but his presence was not that of a twenty-five-year-old at all. It struck me, when he held my back at the tournament and tried to help me with my swing, that he had a presence that was far greater than twenty-five. When he laid his hands on me, it was a strange feeling that I can't quite describe. All I know is that his touch felt warm, familiar, and safe. I remember feeling secure with him next to me that day. It was a weird feeling, so I assumed it was just that I had too much alcohol. The thought of anything other than friendship in the long term was not even a consideration for me because he was too young. He was a perfect guy-friend and I liked that.

After several hours talking and sipping wine, I asked him how tall he was. We both stood up, faced each other, went to measure ourselves, and then we just started to kiss. One thing led to another, but I figured we're both adults, so why not? We had so much fun talking about our hopes and dreams, and we both longed for more real, deep friendships, so we said to each other that we should hang out a lot and become best friends. I was so in! He made me laugh, had great values, shared my goals, was real, and was likely one of the most genuine humans I had ever met.

After he left, in my drunken state, I texted Tom. I wanted him to explain himself. I was back to thinking we would be great together and was hoping that this was somehow just a dumb fight or misunderstanding, and he would tell me there was a perfectly good explanation as to why he was home and hadn't contacted me right away. He came over to my house close to midnight and picked me up in his arms, spinning me around like he was the happiest man on earth. He made me feel like he missed me and couldn't wait to see me. It worked. I was on cloud nine.

He told me that over the summer while he was away, he had finally, after years of being unable to end things, been successful. This time, it was really over. I couldn't believe my ears; I was so excited. I told him I couldn't wait for us to finally date after so long.

The next words I heard come out of his mouth would forever change my life. He looked at me and said that he just needed some time to allow the dust to settle. He told me that he suffered from depression and other personal issues, and it would not be suitable to start a new relationship with me. He said he would still visit me, but that he didn't want to start a relationship yet.

So basically, he would still see me when it was convenient, but he still needed time to figure his life out. Did he not get that I waited in the wings for three years hoping for our moment? His words stung and they caused a knee-jerk reaction that not only would finally close that door, but would slam it shut forever.

I was finally done. I'm not sure how or why this time was different, but somehow it was. Perhaps it was the new self-worth I felt, or the fun life I was living (except when I was waiting for someone who never came). I just snapped and said, "No way," and with that I asked him to leave. As he walked out of the door, I slammed it behind him and felt so relieved and empowered. I wondered why it had taken me so long to have this personal epiphany. Why now? I didn't care. I was just happy to not want him anymore and to suddenly feel my inherent value, as if a mirror was being held in front of my face, and I could finally see it.

I watched him drive off and tried to digest what had just happened. A huge part of my soul felt relief, and I felt so free;

like the shackles of this unhealthy dream were finally cut. I went to bed happy and I trusted myself for the first time in years. I knew I had finally honoured myself for the first time ever and followed my gut. From that moment on, my life has never been the same.

The next morning, I was out on a hike with the dog when my cell phone rang. I looked on the display and saw it was Jesse. He said he was just calling to see how I was feeling. A guy asking me how I was feeling? Really? I was dumbfounded. It was mind blowing, really. I thought to myself, *'Here is this young guy who is actually kind and courteous enough to pick up the phone and call (not text) and ask me how I am!'* I told him I was fine, and when he asked to see me again, I was excited and 100 percent in. I needed to have a friend to hang out with, especially one on my page who could also make me laugh.

The month that followed was so unexpected but spoke to the fact that when one door closes, another one opens. Jesse and I became best friends and as if by accident, lovers, too. We spent hours upon hours soul searching and indulging in deep conversations, drinking wine, and dancing until the wee hours. Just he and I in my rancher laughing, and crying, and discovering the most authentic and real connection that two humans can possibly make.

This connection was not based on money or looks, or what we could gain by being together. It was instead based on us simply grooving on each other in every possible way. I'll never forget when we both realized what was happening: that we were actually falling in love. *'This can't happen'* I remember thinking to myself as Jesse was twenty-five and I was thirty-nine. In fact, Jesse claims to this day that he didn't even know my exact age until I invited him to my 40th birthday party. He thought I was in my early thirties until then, and in all our conversations if just never came up. When I did finally cough and spit out my real age, he didn't flinch. He didn't care at all. He looked me in my eyes and told me he could see us "going yard." I didn't know what that meant, but he explained it was a baseball term and meant going the distance. He said he could picture his life and he meant his entire life, with me.

The next year was a whirlwind of romance. Dinners out, family get-togethers, road trips, parties, dancing, and hours upon hours of deep talks. Within nine months we were engaged, and the rest is history. Our story is one for the books. Our courtship was one of the most beautiful times of my life, perhaps because it was so unplanned and filled with so much self-discovery.

It was the first time I followed my heart, and not my mind. My mind would still chatter away about the pros and cons, but my heart told me not to second guess that connection. I guess he also knew that it was a soul connection. It was a product of two people being in the same place spiritually in their lives, strapped in, and ready to take the roller coaster ride that is life, together without ever looking back.

# CHAPTER THREE

# The Loss

Since I was very small, perhaps around the age of eight, I started to profess to all who would listen about how much I liked to talk. I just loved to talk about anything and everything to anyone who would listen. It's no wonder then that when I fast forward to my life today, I feel so drawn to the idea of being a motivational speaker. It is something that I have said I wanted to do for the past decade, and since I know I can manifest anything I put my mind to, speaking to help others should be no different.

My closest friends remind me of how I used to sip wine with them on our Friday pizza nights and tell them exactly what my life would look like in ten years. I would paint them the magical picture with every last detail. The man I would marry, the son I would have with him and even the black car he would drive. It is truly amazing that all those things I said to them became my reality.

Manifesting the speaking engagements I so desired had not been as simple, however. I strongly remember one day laying on my bed and having another conversation with God. While I felt that being a single mom and having the courage to leave an unhappy marriage and become a real estate agent was indeed an accomplishment worth sharing, that story was too common. Strong women were emerging every day and sharing similar stories, and I didn't want to become another generic story. I remember distinctly saying, "God, please give me a story, one that is unique and inspiring." What I needed was something interesting that would make people pay attention to what I was saying, I thought, something that would draw in an audience. I remember thinking to myself "...just don't give me cancer." Be careful what you wish for.

It was a cold September night in 2014. I went to bed peaceful and grateful for all my many blessings. I woke up around midnight, and as I opened my eyes the ceiling was spinning in circles. It was the scariest experience of my life. I frantically called out for Jesse, who was in a deep sleep beside me. He encouraged me to stand up, but when I did, I immediately fell to the floor. I was experiencing some kind of extreme vertigo. I struggled to make my way to the front door and into the car so we could get to the ER as soon as possible. I was absolutely terrified on the drive over because I could not even sit up without feeling an overwhelming sense of nausea. I thought maybe I had had a stroke, or worse, some kind of brain aneurysm.

When we arrived, I was given a gown and placed into a curtained off cubicle. I lay on my side and kept my eyes tightly shut. The ER doctor examined me for what seemed like an eternity, and finally came back with a diagnosis. He told me that the vertigo was likely caused by a loose crystal in my inner ear. He did a protocol on me called The Epley Maneuver and told me that in five to seven days things should slowly improve. I remember leaving encouraged and totally relieved. When the doctor told me to take it easy, I nervously cracked a joke promising him I would try not to run a marathon. I leaned on Jesse as we exited the ER.

For the next week, I was literally laying horizontal in my bed and taking anti-nausea medications. Each day I woke up just hoping and praying the spinning would stop. The spinning did slowly improve, but as it did, the hearing in my left ear started to feel blocked. It felt like it was waterlogged for some strange reason, out of nowhere at all. Over the next few weeks it got continually worse until I had absolutely no sound whatsoever coming into that ear, as if someone was holding their hand over that hear.

Hoping that this was a routine side effect for the loose crystal I supposedly had, we made an appointment to see my ENT, who, when hearing about my sudden hearing loss, changed my diagnosis very quickly. I now was diagnosed with Labyrinthitis: a virus that affects the inner ear, inflaming the vestibular nerves and causing problems with balance and spatial navigation. Side effects can include vertigo, and *temporary* hearing loss. This should clear up in a matter of weeks, with the hearing in my left ear coming back in full force. Once again, I felt relieved because there was a name for what I was experiencing, and the fact that he labelled my situation as 'temporary.' I was offered steroid medication to help speed up the hearing recovery, but I was afraid because I had always read that steroids can cause serious side effects.

Weeks, and eventually months, went by, and sadly my hearing on the left side never returned. I held out hope for the first few months, but after month three, my ENT told me that the odds of it coming back were almost zero.

The hearing loss was distressing and took a while to adjust to, as I no longer heard sounds coming from my left side. This also meant that I had no more 'surround sound' or ability to echolocate which way the sounds were coming from. What also came along with this affliction was an extreme loss of balance. I was constantly dizzy and nauseated when I stood up. Just trying to walk from my bed to the living room was a huge feat – when I accomplished it. Eventually, as the days passed, I was able to go further. I was able to walk from my bedroom to the kitchen. Then I tried to walk outside. I would set small, incremental daily goals for myself. I would tell Jesse, "Today I walked half a block." Some days I was so angry with my situation that I didn't even want to try. It was easier just to lay flat and not feel dizzy or nauseated. **And just to be angry.**

Jesse would scold me and demand that I stop feeling sorry for myself. He'd tell me that he was taking me across the road to the gravel school field and that I was going to try. I would protest every time and beg him not to make me. The idea of walking all the way across the road to the field was so daunting at the time, but we continued to practice, and I continued to cry while doing so. Sometimes he and Rachael would take the basketball up to the school hoops, and I would challenge myself and walk back and forth in front of them and shout to them to look at me, because I was doing it. Slowly I was regaining my ability to walk. It was far from perfect, and I still staggered at times, but it was becoming more manageable, and I was proud that I had come such a long way.

I used to walk the dog every day for at least an hour. I was militant in my determination to get my dog Flo out and around the neighbourhood every single day. Now I could barely walk across the street without looking like I'd just drunk twelve beers. It was the most challenging experience of my life at that time, relearning to walk. It felt totally surreal to me. It took over six months of hard work and intense rehabilitation to finally feel somewhat able to walk normally without feeling off. By the end I still had difficulty going up and down stairs as my brain was learning a new way to balance, but all-in-all I was at least able to walk, and eventually drive again.

Fast forward to April 2015, our dream destination wedding was only a month away, and planning was in full force. I felt strong again and was finally back doing my one-hour walks, which I affectionately called "The Loop." As I walked, I used that time to clear my mind and visualize things that I wanted to manifest. Since the wedding was weeks away, I would play the song we chose for me to walk down the aisle to on repeat. The song was called "I Choose You," by Sara Bareilles. As I played it, I would literally close my eyes and walk along the sidewalk and visualize myself walking down the aisle. I could feel every emotion that a bride would feel each time I did this. I felt goose-bumps line my arms and tears of joy flow down my face. I felt so much gratitude, and at the same time, disbelief that this was actually finally happening to me. I'd done it! I found my prince! I was the happiest I had ever been, and the fact that I had just spent months working so hard just to walk straight and get used to single-sided deafness made it even more emotional for me.

Exactly three weeks before my wedding day I woke up in the middle of the night and went to the washroom. As I stood up something instantly felt off. I started to feel a bit dizzy again. This was nothing like the vertigo I had experienced that past September, but it certainly was concerning. I called out to Jesse again and told him I thought something was wrong. He assured me that it was likely nothing, and to go to sleep and see how I felt in the morning.

When I woke up in the morning, I was struggling enough just to walk that I called my ENT and asked him what to do. He told me that it was not uncommon to have a relapse some months after the first bout of Labyrinthitis. I was scared, but that made me feel a little better. I was forced to be on bed rest again and take medication to help with the unrelenting spinning sensation and nausea, but at least it was explainable.

On the afternoon of April 16th, and I was lying in my bed coping with the spinning room when Rachael and Jesse came running in to say hello. From the first words they seemed to be talking in really strange voices as if they had just inhaled helium. I asked them why they were talking like Alvin and the Chipmunks. "We're not," they explained to me, "Is everything alright?"

I soon realized that they were talking normally, and it was my hearing that was off. There was some other cause for what I was hearing. Completely panicking, Jesse raced me to the medical clinic where we asked the doctor to look in my ear. We thought that perhaps because I had no hearing on one side, that an ear infection or any injury to the right ear might account for the strange sounds I was hearing. When the doctor saw nothing alarming, we immediately went in to see my ENT, where a hearing test showed I only had 20 percent audible capability left. I was handed a piece of paper and told to go straight to the ER. I was in complete shock at this point and had no idea how this could be happening to me. He had already told me the fact that my hearing didn't return in the left ear was rare, but he had also assured me that I would never lose hearing in the other ear. He likened it to winning the lottery or being struck by lightning… twice.

As I lay on a bed in the overcrowded ER hallway, I listened helplessly to the plethora of sounds in my head; it was not silent at all. Going deaf was ironically not quiet. The sounds were chaotic and hard to hear. They weren't voices anymore, as those had begun to fade. My world as I knew it was collapsing. I was frightened, and despite my fiancé standing beside me, I felt totally alone. As more sounds faded away, I could no longer hear anything at all from the outside world; only the loud thumping… boom-boom, boom-boom… and rushing-water sounds in my head. I was instantly thrust into a world of lip reading as I tried desperately to explain to the doctors what I was hearing inside my head.

Over the next ten days, I became a human guinea pig. I was admitted to the sixth floor of the hospital and had to undergo a battery of tests: CT scans, an MRI, a spinal tap, and dozens of blood tests. Top doctors from all over Vancouver came to assist as sudden deafness was so rare that it was almost unheard of.

I was shuttled off to another hospital to spend hours every day inside a hyperbaric chamber. The chamber was small I was already very claustrophobic. It resembled a large submarine and was located in the dingy, dark basement of a large hospital. Arriving was nerve racking for me; I was given scrubs, anti-anxiety medication, and I had to sign a waiver that I understood that on rare occasions the chamber could explode.

Once inside, I had to wear what I imagine astronauts wear when inside their rockets. It was a special face mask that delivered oxygen, and only added to the claustrophobia. The door would shut and ten of us, all with hearing loss, would sit side by side and look at a movie overhead. Our group chaperone would spin the wheel and seal us all in, pressurizing the cabin. We would have timed sessions with the mask on, then take it off, then back on again, and off again, for the duration of our visit. Once the submarine reached a certain level of pressure you couldn't panic and want to leave as it took a long time to depressurize again. Just knowing that made one more likely to panic and want to get out. I was also pumped full of steroid medication that the doctors hoped would help bring my hearing back, which also didn't help my nerves.

I hated the idea of being on steroids. I was so claustrophobic in the chamber. I was terrified of the needle going in my spine during the spinal tap they thought might help diagnose me. I endured it. I took the steroids. I had no other choice. This was it.

I was going to be deaf if I wasn't going to be brave.

By some miracle, after seven days, my hearing began to return. It was not perfect, but it was enough to allow me to hear voices again and talk on my phone. 'I'll take it!' I thought. Beggars can't be choosers, and after going a week without sound, or worse still, just hearing these irritating noises, I felt I had averted disaster and I knew how lucky I was.

My therapies were obviously working, and just in time for my upcoming wedding. I was blown up like a balloon from the steroids, I had the classic steroid 'moon face,' which was covered in pimples, but I could hear something, so I didn't care. I thought to myself at least I would go on to hear my groom say, "I do," so it was ok to be a puffy and pimple faced bride, as long as I could hear—or so I thought.

Days after being released from the hospital, I was given a hearing test and told I had about 70 percent audible capability left in one ear. I accepted that and felt it was definitely far better than where I was a week earlier. I was still so dizzy, every bone in my body hurt, and my balance was off again, but somehow, I knew I needed to soldier on and make it to my wedding in a few weeks.

It was the weekend of my bachelorette party, and I was on a set tapering schedule to get off the steroid medication. I was also given a drug called Ativan to help me deal with the anxiety of handling my hearing loss and my upcoming wedding. On that Friday, my hearing started to decline again. I was in utter denial. I had truly believed that what came back was what I would be left with. Terrified, I promptly visited the ENT, where they put me in the booth several times over the next twenty-four hours, and each time I went in the result became more dire. It had dropped from seventy percent to sixty, then to fifty, then to forty, and then they sent me next door to be fitted with a hearing aid.

When your hearing percentage and range falls below a certain level, there is still a chance to amplify it with a hearing aid, but no one prepared me for how that sounds. It was surreal to say the least.

When I walked into the clinic, I could barely make out a word the audiologist was saying to me. He placed the device over my right ear, with a small portion sitting inside. He turned it on, and it indeed amplified the sound and helped me to hear much better. It was somewhat relieving, until I stepped outside and heard the reverberation. I could hear crazy ringing sounds and strange noises as I approached and passed certain buildings. I ran back inside and said that I thought something was wrong with the device, but they told me that it was just some of the unfortunate quirks associated with certain hearing aids. It was so depressing and so hard to wrap my head around. All I was worried about at the time was whether the percentage of detectable sound in my right ear was going to keep dropping. I only had so much volume I could increase, and then I would be out of luck.

On the night of my bachelorette party I did my best to stay positive and dress myself for dinner with the ladies, despite only wanting to crawl into bed. I couldn't even be bothered with applying a drop of makeup. I arrived at my favorite restaurant and struggled to present myself, even to my closest friends, with my new hearing issues. I felt shame for some reason, like I was different now. I could barely hear the waiter speaking to me, even with the hearing aid, because I was, after all, only hearing with an amplified 40 percent on one side and total deafness on the left. I struggled through dinner, straining to catch parts of conversations here and there. I was too nauseated and dizzy from steroid withdrawal to eat or drink much.

After dinner was over, I leaned in to my dear friend Kim and asked her if she could kindly walk me to my car as I didn't trust my wobbly gait. I linked arms with her, and we made our way. I think I cried the whole way home. I had never felt so alone in my entire life. Even though I had friends and family to talk to, no one was me at that time, sinking further and further into an abyss. It was one thing to be going deaf, but quite another to not know why any of it was happening. The timing of that weekend made things far worse, as Jesse was away on his stag weekend with his friends, and so I was physically alone, too. I remember lying in bed feeling my hearing diminish hour by hour, until I could no longer turn it up anymore. Jesse was partying and drinking, so I barely heard from him that weekend. He didn't realize I was going deaf while he was away.

I Facetimed my mom and I told her that I could no longer hear. I opened and shut my bedside drawer all night hoping I would hear something, but all I felt was the vibrations of things. In desperation, my mom drove me to the hearing aid place, where we frantically explained my situation. He put me in his hearing booth, and I sat with the clicker waiting to press it when I heard a sound. I never did press it. He sat me down and mouthed the words "I'm sorry." He said he needed to take his hearing aid back. He took it off my ear and said that it would no longer be of any use to me. He said I did not have enough hearing left to make use of an aid and that my only option going forward would be a cochlear implant.

A part of me died that day. I said goodbye to natural hearing and the idea of ever having it again. I also said goodbye to my old way of life. I lived a life where I loved to talk, but I never really loved to listen, and now all I wanted to do was listen but was unable to do so. God had a plan for me, and it was extremely difficult to comprehend, but I did ask for a story, and boy did I get one.

# CHAPTER FOUR

# The Wedding

The aftermath of being told I was a deaf person at the mid-point in my life was definitely not something I could have prepared for. It was as if my life was a piece of paper and someone came in and crumpled it up and then gave me a blank page and said, "start again." I remember the long, sweltering hot days leading up to the wedding, lying on my bed completely dizzy and deaf, forced to listen to unrelenting loud sounds spiraling around in my head. On top of that, I experienced the deepest sense of fear I've ever felt.

You see, as I was going through the gradual hearing loss, I still held out so much hope that being actually deaf was likely never going to happen. It just seemed way too far-fetched, and in the life I had always visualized for myself, being deaf was just not part of it. I was sent so many books from kind well-wishers about how to think yourself healed and the power of the mind, so I spent hours each day immersed in those books, assuming that God would flick on the hearing switch just in time for my big day. For some reason, I held on to that hope basically right up until we said, "I do."

It was the dreaded day. I say dreaded because it meant I had to actually get out of bed, and despite being dizzy, nauseated, and post-steroid pimple faced, I had to man up and put on a brave front. We loaded up the car and drove five hours into the interior of beautiful British Columbia, where our wedding at the Harvest Golf Course in the quaint lake town of Kelowna was to take place. The wedding was set in stone. Flights were booked for all our relatives from back east and other destinations; there was no turning back.

The long drive up was scenic and I daydreamed through the whole car ride. It was my first long ride during which I couldn't hear a musical note, a human voice, or even the car engine. It was the start of my new world where each moment was filled with so much self-discovery that it was exhausting. As I gazed out the window, I looked at the familiar landscapes and all that would come to me was how I wished I could have appreciated the drive more last time I came here, because last time I could still hear.

My mind was racing about all the details we had spent six months preparing for. What was going to happen at the meet and greet party? Only a handful of people knew I was deaf at this point. How would I be able to communicate with all the guests? What would they be thinking about poor Jesse, a young healthy man, about to commit his life to a deaf woman 15 years older than him? There was so much more at work here than just living in silence; it was also the impact my doing so would have on all those around me.

It was the 5th of June 2015. We arrived at The Manteo Waterfront Resort; a lovely hotel we'd handpicked months before when we drove out to plan our dream day. As we stepped into the scorching heat, my dizzy body struggled to maintain the upright position. 'Ok, I got this.' I said to myself as I made my way behind my fiancé. In the distance our relatives were waving us down, not expecting to be met with the shocking news we were about to tell them. The funny thing was that my main concern was not 'Will I be okay?' but 'Will they be okay now that I can't hear? Will they still accept me, or will they pull Jesse aside and try to talk some sense into him?'

As the hot day melted into night, it was time for the makeup artist to do a run through with me. I had been so excited months earlier for this night, knowing that I would get all 'Hollywood Glammed' up for the meet and greet, and then also get a glimpse of what the wedding day makeup might look like. I was, again, so nervous about how the makeup artist would handle my deafness, as I knew she had spoken excitedly on the phone to me not three weeks earlier. She would be shocked, and I would feel awkward telling her my story. I just wanted everyone to know, to just get it over with, so the elephant could stand freely, front and centre in the room.

I'll never forget the disbelief that kept circulating like a toxin through my mind. It can't be, but no, this is my wedding. No, I can't believe this. I can't handle this. It's not possible.... The mind chatter was relentless, and it only heightened my fear and anxiety. I felt so much better telling people that I had just suffered temporary hearing loss, even if I didn't believe it myself. The story was comforting to everyone else, so I stuck with that. It gave them hope when they looked at me, and perhaps even gave me a tiny bit of false hope, too. Just enough to get me through.

I stumbled around the meet and greet and focused hard on walking straight, so I didn't look drunk to my guests. Of course, when you're dizzy and stumbling, you'd rather not be the centre of attention. I had at least one major panic attack when I was sitting in a chair just chatting with my dad and fiancé. I began to sweat, my heart started to pound, and I knew then that the steroid withdrawal had a mind of its own, which was not about to allow me any graces.

When the meet and greet party was over, I was sadly relieved. For me, it was work, and I mean really hard work! I had to try to walk straight, welcome my guests, and then spend hours dizzy, trying to make conversation by exercising my newly discovered lip-reading skills. What a whirlwind! I was totally mentally exhausted. I had instantly aged thirty years and needed to get my grandma ass into bed, especially if I hoped to be getting married the next day.

That night, the idea of sleep was pretty much a pipe dream. Imagine what thoughts would be going through your mind. It wasn't just the fear and anxiety of how I would hear and say my vows, but also the steroid and Ativan withdrawal, which was relentless and caused heart palpitations, sweating, and a near constant state of panic. The timing was not good for me, but as I said earlier, the show must go on!

I may have finally managed to close my eyes around 4 am and was awoken by a stream of sunlight beaming through the partially open drape. I stumbled over to our lakeside balcony and wandered out to take in the sight. It occurred to me, right then and there, how much more beautiful the sights appeared, now that I had lost the sounds. Wow! It was such a beautiful land-scape I was blessed with seeing, and to think just beside me was my loving fiancé, whose only mission these days was to ensure my comfort. All of a sudden, I felt lucky. Yes, lucky! I was going to marry my true love; a love that didn't care a bit if his wife would be unable to hear him speak again. He wanted me and only me. I could see the lake and all the beauty around me, and it filled me with happiness. Somehow, then, I knew I would be ok. I would walk down the aisle and face all of my fears head on.

As I stood in the foyer of the clubhouse, I could see the lush, green golf course below me. I was so aware of all the senses that I still had that the smell of fresh cut grass was almost a bit over-whelming. The scene was like being in a 3D cartoon movie. All the colours were so much brighter than what I remembered be-fore, and the lake in the background, combined with the weep-ing willow trees and water fountains, just left me spellbound. I was inside a fairytale and that fairytale was so perfect that the artist that created it didn't leave out a single brush stroke.

I was led down the long concrete staircase, handed my overly-fragrant bouquet, and directed to my starting position. The wedding planner was geared up and ready to push me forward on cue. She looked a little sweaty knowing she had a bride who couldn't hear the wedding march, but she seemed confident nonetheless.

I grabbed my dad's arm, closed my eyes, and thought of my tingling arms on the sidewalk of the loop I used to walk.

Suddenly, as if by magic, I was hearing Sara Bareilles sing a private concert in my head. "I Choose You" played in perfect harmony for my guests to hear as I walked determinedly next to my Dad. The song also played in perfect harmony for me because I had visualized it so many times before. How miraculous was that? Was that all a coincidence? It was a beautiful moment in my life that cannot ever be forgotten. At that moment in time, as I clumsily walked toward my prince, who was beaming with pride, I felt like I was the luckiest woman on the earth. I knew that our love was unconditional, and that it was a love so powerful, only my creator could have had his divine hands on it. This was a story to be written about; a destined love and the witnessing of a bond so deep that it would be etched in earthly history forever.

I found myself holding the warm hand of my Jesse. His beautiful, soulful eyes were where I held my gaze. He mouthed the words 'I do', and 'forever', and that was all I needed to see. The rest was just a feeling. I repeated my vows on cue and read from a tiny crumpled page I had handwritten the night before. As I looked around, I saw my daughter crying buckets of tears beside me. She was my sensitive little girl, and her soulfulness was evident that day as she absorbed so much love being exchanged between us. The guests all told me afterward how they had never been more emotionally charged at a wedding because they knew the depth of the struggle, and the true love that was being expressed before them.

The wedding played out exactly as it should, or shall I say, as I had imagined. I was somehow able to lip read all the speeches and actually understand them. I even delivered my own very powerful speech. The DJ played, and I felt the vibrations of the bass as the guests twirled around, high on life, and of course, a selection of the finest spirits. When it came time for our first song as husband and wife, I was overcome with emotion, because I really wanted to hear Ed Sheeran sing "Thinking Out Loud." This was our song; it felt made for us. Just as I began wishing, Jesse clasped my hand and met my gaze. Then he began mouthing the words to the entire song for me as he gently twirled me around the dance floor. Out there in the night, my world was silent. I heard not a sound, but I felt the voice of love resonate deep within the belly of my soul. If this was what going deaf did for me, then in that moment, frozen in time, I would forever be grateful.

## CHAPTER FIVE

# Another Miracle

I think it was the late 80's when George Michael had a steady influence in my life. His music was everywhere, and the one song that I used to play on repeat was oddly making its presence known again in my head, "Faith." When you have no more sounds to take for granted, you are grateful for the old songs that randomly pop up and disrupt the usual annoying mind chatter. It was curious that a song I hadn't really heard in three decades chose to play on repeat, but I took note of the title and in my usual fashion, looked at it as a sign. Something, somewhere, was with me on this ride, and that something was comforting me, and somehow telling me to hang in there.

After we came back from the wedding, reality quickly began to set in. Everyone went about their lives, as per usual, and the excitement and the build-up of our big day was slowly becoming a distant memory. As the summer days grew hotter and longer, my struggles seemed to become amplified. I was totally displaced. When I thought about getting back to work, I realized I couldn't because I wouldn't be able to hear my clients. Then I realized I couldn't talk to my friends because I can't hear on the phone. TV and movies...? Nope, I couldn't hear them. Even a therapist couldn't talk to me, because I wouldn't be able to listen to them. It was a huge mess in my mind. I was absolutely shell shocked. It started hitting me that everything I used to love was no longer a real possibility for me. I could never just listen to music or drive with the radio on, hear a horn honk or the wail of an ambulance. What about an intruder or a fire alarm? It was the scariest and most depressing few months of my entire life. It was a long hot summer, and I was caught in a place where I had no idea what was about to become of my life. Who was going to help me? How was I to find my way? Would I hear ever again? Oh, how I wished I had listened to the last song I ever heard more closely, or the sweet sound of my daughter's voice.

I spent a good portion of my days doing research on the web and visiting various doctors, still holding out some faint hope that somehow, miraculously, we would figure out what caused my hearing loss and fix it. One of the things my ENT kept telling me was, "It's ok, Monique. The worst-case scenario is you can always get a cochlear implant." *What the hell is that?* I remember thinking. *An implant?* I peppered him with every imaginable question, that poor man, but unfortunately, his answers were not pleasing to me. The sounds, he told me, would not be like normal hearing. It would sound much more robotic. In fact, he shared that each person perceives the sound differently, and some are only able to hear beeps and buzzes.

Beeps and buzzes? Was he serious? I researched the implant and saw this hideous device that sticks to your scalp somehow with a magnet and connects to a big fat hearing aid device that sits on your ear. This device was not discreet. It looked big and bulky, and to top it off, the sound I might get from it was less than appealing. I wondered why anyone would get that, and I dug my heels in. I was so reluctant to cut up my ear and attempt to place this implant, because that would then guarantee I would never have natural hearing ever again. My left ear was already eight months deaf and I knew it wasn't coming back, but I still held out hope that the right one was going to surprise me, since it had only been two months.

The MRI, unfortunately, made my decision for me. The news was not good. I was told by the doctor that my left ear showed significant ossification on the scan, which meant that whatever disease, process, or virus that had been there left a trail of thick scar tissue inside my cochlea when it retreated. This scar tissue replaced the fluid and the eight thousand tiny hairs that acted as communicators by sending little signals to my brain. I was told that trying to place an implant through that amount of scarring was near impossible, and so attempting to implant my left ear was not a possibility. The scan showed my right ear, after two short months, was already starting the ossification process, and so waiting to implant me was not an option either. If I waited, I would be too scarred on that side, too, and would run the risk of having no implant at all. I couldn't wait another day to decide; it was instantaneous. The two year wait list was waived for me, as my condition was considered dire at this point. It was rare to find a woman in her prime with a successful career and a child that suddenly and randomly went deaf. They knew that if they didn't act fast that I would be out of luck.

When they laid my options out in front of me, the bulky, ugly, possibly robotic sounding device suddenly became appealing. 'Beggars can't be choosers' came to mind as I quickly signed the paperwork to get the process started. I somehow began to feel excited that I was getting some help. I felt that there was a little light at the end of the tunnel. Some people who'd had it had been able to return to work, and it was encouraging that there were top lawyers who had cochlear implants. Some people even learned to use the phone again with this implant, so I began to ask myself, *why couldn't that be me?*

I sat for two hours, beaming with pride as the doctors at the hospital interviewed me in a kind of psychological fashion, ensuring that I really and truly understood what to expect when the device they were about to implant into my head was switched on. For this entire two hour meeting they couldn't believe that I could read their lips and answer so quickly without needing them to type what they were saying on the computer screen. No sir, not for me... I had become a lip-reading master, and I was proud of that skill. It was rather miraculous that I was able to sit through two hours of psychological and medical conversation and stay right on top of every word.

I got to choose the colour of my exterior device; I selected beige to blend best with my blonde hair. They showed me all the fancy covers I could order which seemed outrageous at the time, because all I thought to myself was, "why the hell would I want to draw attention to this thing that was going to be stuck to the side of my head?" I just wondered how I would need to wear my hair to best hide the device.

I left that meeting feeling as excited as a person could possibly be. I decided then and there that my outcome would be one of the good ones. That I would be able to hear like the top lawyers, and I'd be able to learn to use the phone again, too. I dreamed about working once more as a realtor and going back out into the world; really living. Imagine that! I saw so many possibilities all of a sudden, and nothing had really changed, except I began to have faith.

# CHAPTER SIX

# The Operation

It was July 27, 2015, and my surgery day had finally come. After many countdown videos and posts on Facebook, I now had a team of people supporting me, and that support proved invaluable. Social media and the web were all I had during my three months of total silence, and so it was a comfort for me going into surgery to read the hundreds of comments wishing me the best possible outcome.

I posed in my blue scrubs and put on a brave face as I stood in front of the locker I was assigned. This wasn't even an overnight stay. No, they would cut my head open behind my ear, try to thread the electrodes though my semi-ossified cochlea and then attach a magnet encased in a safe material to my scalp, sew me back up and then, once my vitals were all good, I was supposed to go home.

I was absolutely terrified. The thoughts that went through my mind were not calm ones. I was thinking about all the risks, like getting meningitis or them not being able to get the electrodes in. The negative mind chatter did not help me that morning, but as I lay with butterflies in my stomach, I knew that this was an all-or-nothing event for me. I had no choice but to go in and get this done. No matter what the outcome, I needed to try.

I said goodbye to Jesse, and they wheeled me down the large hallway into the surgery room. It was cold and very bright, and these massive alien-like lamps shone down on me. Doctors and nurses flew around me preparing the room. One walked over to me and placed a mask over my face, and I was out.

When I awoke, I was greeted by a lovely nurse offering to inject me with more pain medication, which I happily accepted. I felt totally disoriented and had some mild stabbing pains around my head. The news was given to me as quickly as I was able to comprehend it; the doctor was able to get the implant in past the scar tissue! That was all I could have hoped for at that time. We wouldn't know how well it would work or what sounds I may or may not hear for three long weeks. I had to allow everything to heal, and for the swelling to come down before they would attempt to place the external components of the implant on and test the electrodes. But it was in!

August 18, 2015. That was the day that, if I was lucky, I would be able to hear sound again. Sound; just sound, whatever that was, would be better than what I had. I was so excited in those warm weeks leading up to my 'switch on.' I had my social media friends counting the days with me, and I had adapted to a certain degree within my new life of hearing nothing. Communication was done by reading lips and being forthright with people about my condition. If I went to Starbucks, I simply looked at the barista and said, "I have temporary hearing loss and I can't hear a sound, so please bear with me." Most people were intrigued and comforting; willing to assist. I felt loved and cared for, and had a totally new appreciation for life. I started to see my cup as half-full again because I saw all the good that could come from something that, just a few months prior, seemed dire. I saw that most people are really good and have loving hearts, and if you reach out and ask, they most often want to help you. The comfort in that is the feeling of no longer being alone. I learned that I could easily have sunk into the deep, dark abyss of depression, which would have meant my ego-mind and its chatter would have won, but that would have been an easy way out. I found another way out, and it was far better than I possibly could have imagined.

All it took was time for me to realize that with or without hearing, I was still living. I had found hope because maybe the 'switch on' would bring me some sound, and though the truth was that I didn't know what kind of sound I would hear, I still decided to go out and start living again. I soon saw that I could still have conversations; I just had to lip read the answers. I could still watch movies; my brain just learned to read the captions. I could still see and, magically, those colors became brighter. Food tasted better. I still had my husband, my family, and all my friends. My career was a concern, but thankfully Jesse was a realtor too, so he took on the business. With his efforts and positive attitude, he almost tripled our business — the year I went deaf!

Miracles were happening everywhere around me, and I started to realize that this all had to have purpose and deeper meaning. I began to see that, perhaps, I was lucky to have this happen because it gave me the chance in this life to reawaken my senses and really appreciate my many blessings. I started to feel alive again and came to the realization that I was living before, but maybe not fully. I was going through the motions, as we all so often do. We wake up, kiss our spouse goodbye, and walk out the door, grumbling about how there will likely be so much traffic or that our job or the weather sucks. We work our eight-hour shift, clock out, then come home exhausted and sit in the easy chair, microwave some food, watch a show or surf on our tablets, and then we're off to bed. I call that existing, but I don't call that living. I'm certain that is not thriving the way we were meant to here on earth. We are meant to have joy and take in the wonder of daily life and all the gifts it can offer. How we perceive things changes everything, and I learned that firsthand.

There I was, still just as deaf as I had been two months earlier, but I was running around happier than ever because I had made a choice that no matter what, I could still live my life. Yes, it was forced upon me. I had no choice but to attempt the surgery and that prospect did help, but I still needed to get up and decide that no matter the outcome, it was up to me to decide how I wanted to live going forward. Would I let this break me?

The weekend before my 'switch on' we had planned a family vacation to Whistler because my brother was in town from Japan. I was so excited to enjoy a few nights of relaxation with my family in anticipation of my big day. I really wanted to make sure that my story was published in the local papers and on the news because sudden deafness is not common, especially at forty-one years old with no prior history of hearing issues. It was very important that my story be shared so I could offer hope to another person who may have had, or who might suffer in the future, a similar fate.

The news media was set to bring their cameras in to St. Paul's Hospital and capture the moment when I would hear sound again for the first time after three months of silence. The world would be there with me to see the joy on my face and hopefully spread the word about the miracle of a cochlear implant and the hope it could offer someone else. I was so happy to be able to share this big event with the world.

The day before my holiday though, I received a call from the surgeon's office that they wanted to talk to me urgently before my procedure. I was concerned by this phone call and insisted they get me in within a few hours. I did not want to leave for my trip with so much worry. When we arrived at St. Paul's Hospital, my heart was pounding out of my chest as I was led down the hall to the audiologist's office. It was there that the most heart-sinking message was delivered to me. As she spoke the words to me, it was as if I left my body, and this world, temporarily. I was not really there. She mouthed the words to me slowly and as she delivered them, my hopes and dreams seemed to fall to the floor once again.

She started by telling me that she thought that CTV news should not be present during my 'switch on.' Prior to this, the hospital had been thrilled to have the coverage and exposure. This change was alarming, so I knew when I asked for their reason it was not going to be good. It seems that after they place the electrodes during surgery and the patient is fast asleep, they are somehow able to test the system and see how your brain responds. This allows them to get a rough gauge as to how many of the twenty-two electrodes might be working and thus be able to deliver sound. They said that when they tested me, all twenty-two were not working, and that they would hate for any disappointment to occur that day and for it be captured live for the world to see. Right away I asked how many were working for me, and the response was so disheartening. Seven. Only seven of the twenty-two were shown to be operational while I lay sleeping post-op. Seven.

*How could that be?* I was beside myself with grief. I felt that my chances of being a "Super Hearer" and showing the world what I was able to do were fading to nothing. I left defeated, with my tail planted firmly between my legs. My weekend was filled with anxiety as I awaited the outcome. My excitement had turned to fear, but there was still one tiny thread of hope. They told me that sometimes the test they perform is not accurate, and they had seen occasions when all the electrodes work at 'switch on,' despite the test saying otherwise. I tried my best to keep my mind focused on that chance, but it sure wasn't easy.

The weekend in Whistler was time well spent, but it could not have ended fast enough. At this point, I was done with waiting, and I wanted the moment of truth to arrive. As we drove over the Lions Gate Bridge, I remember trembling with fear and anticipation, and delivering a monologue to Jesse. I say monologue because I was not looking at his lips to gain a response. I just wanted to talk out all the nervousness.

We arrived, and my heart raced as we were directed into the audiologist's office. She began to explain the process of listening and hearing sound. It's hard for anyone to imagine what that means to a person who can hear absolutely nothing, not even their own voice. To me, a sound was a miracle at that point, so even a beep or a buzz would be welcome. As she turned on the machine to begin her test, she told me not to panic if I heard nothing at first. I thought, 'Geez.... She thinks I'm stupid. She is preparing me for the dead electrodes. Of course I am going to panic.'

Her hand would wave, and after that I was supposed to hear a sound. If her hand waved and I didn't, I would surely panic. Her first wave began, and thankfully that one was followed by a blessed beep. WOW! I heard a beep; a sound! It was super exciting and very odd. How could I hear something? I was deaf. Then she raised her hand again, and another beep came, but it had a different tone. Then again, and again, she raised her hand, and I enjoyed beep after beep. It was a symphony to me. After a few minutes, she mouthed to me that she would now switch me on.

The 'switch on' came, and what I could hear was the strangest and weirdest collection of noises. The sounds were her talking, but it sounded like a robot and I could not make out the words. Then Jesse spoke and Rachael spoke, and they all sounded the same as Heather. No change in tone in their voices at all. Slowly, they began to sound less robotic. Then I tried to tap, and I heard a collection of noises when I spoke. I, too, sounded like they did. After ten minutes, we started to all sound like Alvin and the Chipmunks. It was very strange.

After a few more minutes, my brain began to make some sense of the stimulation, and words began to sound like words. I said, "Necessarily" and heard myself say it. I jumped out of my chair and asked if I just said 'necessarily'. As I asked, I jumped again, wide-eyed, as I realized I had not only said it again but knew for sure that I'd heard myself say it! It was astonishing! I could already hear speech! They had told me that I may only hear beeps and buzzes for months or maybe that's all I would ever hear, but I was hearing words within twenty minutes! It was strange that we all sounded the same, but she assured me that that would change over time.

I looked at her and asked the big, scary question, which was, "How many electrodes actually worked?" and she flashed two hands with five fingers on each at me, which meant ten. Then she did it again! So, twenty? Then she held up two more fingers and had a huge grin!! "You mean twenty-two?" I asked, and with that, we all stood up and jumped around the room. It was a miracle! I could hear again, and all twenty-two electrodes were working. I could leave happy and start my new journey, experiencing each day how my brain would adapt to my miracle device.

# CHAPTER SEVEN

# Life After Deaf

The excitement of finally hearing something after months of silence was obviously tantalizing. There would be so many things to learn and a lot of troubleshooting initially with the implant. I never thought about the fact that I couldn't sleep with the implant on, as it would not be comfortable, and it could damage the skin on my head over time from all the pressure. That meant at night I would need to rely on others' ears to protect me from harm. I would not be able to hear smoke alarms, telephones, or any other urgent situations, should they arise.

The implant was a work in progress for me for the first three months, especially as it had my brain working overtime. I would hear a sound and have no idea what it was until someone told me. *Oh, that's a dog barking, or a bird chirping… or that's the water running.* It was crazy to hear noises but not know what those noises were. I also had a single sided implant, so I had no concept of which direction the sounds were coming from, and that in itself presented its own set of challenges.

I was told that during the first three months, the changes in my hearing quality would skyrocket and then level off, with improvements still occurring up to three years later, but those would be much more subtle. As the first weeks passed, I was starting to hear my family again in all their glory. So instead of everyone sounding like female chipmunks, they began to sound like their old selves. My mom's German accent was back, and the sweet sound of my daughter's voice also returned. It was such an amazing experience to witness the miracle of the human brain and exactly what it was capable of.

I remembered a time in the heat of the summer when I was lying on my bed slowly going deaf. I would reach over to my dresser drawer and open it, then shut it to ensure that I could at least still hear that noise, or I would walk over to the blinds and run my nails down them to see if I could hear it. I had these desperate routines and rituals I would follow between reading books on how to self-heal, along with saying my prayers. God and I had a thing. I would say, *"Please, just let me hear the birds chirp still."* That was one of my measures of how much I could still hear. I would lay still, slow my breathing, grasp the covers and lay in wait. Then... by some miracle, or so it would seem back then, I would hear a chirp. It was a message to me from God, and it never failed to give me comfort.

When I lost all my hearing and I could no longer hear the birds, I would pray for the return, someday, of their beautiful chirps. Seven months after surgery, my mom and I were enjoying a conversation up high on her balcony, taking in the ocean views. It was a glorious spring day and we caught a glimpse of two birds dancing in front of us. Suddenly a little miracle occurred: I heard them chirping away. Their sweet sounds sent tears of joy streaming down my face and my mother's eyes also filled with tears when she realized what was happening. For her to witness so much happiness from her daughter; to hear a sound that everyone else took for granted every day surely had an impact on her. It also had a lasting impact on me. I knew on some level then, that everything would be ok, but that was my communication with God. That was his message to me. It took time, but it was a miracle and certainly worth the wait.

Along with the joys of hearing more sounds each day came some sad and very sobering realities. The first big one was that I couldn't listen to music anymore; I was not prepared for that. I thought if I practiced listening, my brain would eventually sort it out. To this day, it has not happened. Music sounds like noise to me. It certainly is not something that I would seek out to deliberately listen to. The TV was also unclear, as each voice was different, and men's voices seem easier than women's for me to hear. So that meant movies were out also. It was all difficult for me to accept. Recently, we discovered a captioning device that fits in your drink holder at the theatre, so movies are back on, but I have to read my way through. I also learned to watch TV by reading the captions. It actually became a habit for my brain, and now I can really enjoy TV again; I don't even seem to notice that I'm reading. The human brain is amazing and can adapt to even the most challenging situations when combined with human will. The telephone was hard to deal with because not hearing perfectly meant that I couldn't call up my clients with confidence and have a conversation about work. I thought that would come faster, but it wasn't coming fast enough. I couldn't call a friend and just chat about life, kids; well anything really. I could only use email or text.

I could hear well face to face, but the person's voice had to be aimed toward me, and at a reasonable distance. If someone spoke behind me or at my deaf side, the chances were good that I couldn't hear them clearly. This left with a huge predicament. How would I be able to be independent?

I would not feel safe at night alone without Jesse. I could not safely do an open house alone because I couldn't hear which way the sound was coming from. I also couldn't hear multiple people asking questions, especially from across the room. My confidence began to shrink as I started to see the real limitations and handicaps that I would face in my life going forward.

Even after such joy, I felt very alone and almost like my world was closing in again. The walls between me and my dreams seemed to grow thicker and thicker. I longed to go out and sell real estate again; talk on the phone, listen to The Eagles. None of that was going to happen, and I had to learn quickly to adapt and accept this new life that, after forty-one years, was thrust upon me.

It was tough because the reality is, I was one of the lucky ones and obviously was blessed to have been given a second chance to hear. I was not in a wheelchair. I was not blind. I did not have a disease with only months to live. I knew better than to allow my mind to bring me down into an abyss, but sometimes knowing better isn't enough.

I became isolated and reluctant to go do the things I used to enjoy. I started to wonder why my husband would want to stay with me when, once a powerful top-selling realtor, I had become almost no help at all to him in our business. I was a shell of my former outgoing and outspoken self, and most days I shed tears as I tried to navigate my way through the sadness.

I wanted my life back, and because the dust had settled and I wasn't where I thought I should be, I let my sadness get the better of me. It became apparent that I needed time to grieve my old life and that an element of post-traumatic stress was coming into play because for the past year I had been in a constant state of fight-or-flight as my hearing loss dominated my life. It was like a hurricane coming in and demolishing my home and taking with it every ounce of evidence that I ever lived there: my photos, my music collection, my work awards, and even my clothing. I was looking at mud and dirt, and now I needed to cultivate the land. I would need to rebuild my home from the ground up and refurnish it to suit the new me. I didn't want to be handicapped but hearing loss to me was a silent handicap. I was displaced in society and even in my own home, and I needed a radical plan to integrate myself into a new life. I knew that it wasn't going to happen overnight.

# Chapter Eight

# Divine Timing

Jesse and I had talked about wanting to start a family together, and when I say that, I don't mean to say that he, Rachael, and I were not already a family, but we wanted to co-create a life together. When we met, I was thirty-nine and I knew that with him being twenty-five, he would one day want some children of his own. However, that one day couldn't be too far away, because my biological clock was ticking, so the important conversation needed to be had early on.

Since the hearing loss fiasco took up the majority of our first year of marriage, when the dust finally settled in early 2016, we decided to look closely at conceiving a baby. Shortly before we met, I had gone for a fertility review, and after extensive testing, I realized that getting pregnant on my own was not going to be easy as my egg count was fairly low. I sought the counselling and guidance of a fertility clinic in Vancouver, and they told me the best bet for us would be IVF (in vitro fertilization).

At first, I was reluctant and scared of the whole process. I was to take an excessive amount of hormone medication, among other not-so-enticing, not to mention invasive, testing procedures. We didn't try the natural route for long before we just decided that if this baby was to become a reality, we'd better get down to business.

The process itself should not be Googled. In fact, I will say that most medical procedures should not be Googled, as it is more than likely that those who author the reviews either: a) had an uber-exciting experience, or b) nearly died. Those are your posters; not your average Joe who has a typical uneventful procedure.

I was a medical Googler after the sudden deafness because I was desperate to self-diagnose since no one else could. The honest truth is that fertility drugs are a bit messy, and not always convenient to 'install', and the hormone swings are no fun for the spouse – that's for sure! A few of the procedures, like seeing if your tubes are all clear, are unpleasant, but in the end I found that I had worked myself up for nothing nine times out of ten.

I'm not sure if I believe in luck as much as I believe in fate. Especially after suddenly going completely deaf one month before my fairytale wedding to my dream man; something that I had visualized since I was a little girl.

Fate is a funny thing. The odds of having a successful embryo creation that then leads to a live birth are not super high. So many factors would need to come into play to end up with our little baby; the baby that I somehow knew I was going to have well before I met Jesse. I had told my friends and family that one day, when I did finally meet my future Mr. Right, we would surely have a son named Jack.

After taking the hormones exactly as I was told to do, the big day finally arrived. The ultrasound that I'd had two days prior, showed that my uterine lining was thick and fluffy; welcoming for our little embryo. Apparently, we'd made two, and they were Grade A. I wondered how the doctor selected which one was to be inserted but that was up to fate.

Jesse and I danced around the waiting room making jokes and squealing with laughter as we put on our scrubs in preparation for the transfer. It was a day we had spent several years planning, and it was so surreal to us that in a week we could actually be pregnant.

I was prepared and lay on the table. A large screen, much like a projection screen, was lit up, and we were shown a blown-up version of our embryo. The doctor went into another room and then prepared the syringe, much like a turkey baster, for the transfer. The end of the "baster" had a trigger which Jesse was going to pull, so it was all very official. When she returned, I was told to relax, despite feeling anything but.

We counted down and then, just like that, the trigger was pulled, and we were told we could leave. I remember feeling like I shouldn't be standing for fear that it would cause the embryo to fall out. We left the clinic and talked about what had just happened. Somehow, we just expected that it would work out for us. Perhaps we felt we deserved some things to finally go our way after all the bumps in our road.

The one-week wait was horrendous. It was impossible to relax. Every waking minute I wanted to pee on a stick, but I knew that peeing too early would only give me a false negative. I think the wait is supposed to be fourteen days, but after seven I decided to check. I stared at that stick and time stood still, but there it was. As if by magic, I saw a tiny faint pink line. It was so faint that I truly had to strain to see it, but I knew that the line wouldn't appear if the hormone was not in my body. I screamed excitedly. Jesse lay sleeping, and when I told him he basically shrugged it off, not really believing me and thinking I was nuts because it was only seven days, and he couldn't even see the line. I knew though. I was certain, and the miracle of it all hit home for me. I was forty-two and pregnant!

# Chapter Nine

# Meeting Jack

As we settled into the reality that we were nine months away from meeting our baby, we began preparations for where said baby would sleep. The third bedroom in our rancher was serving as our family home theatre/rec room, and we needed to convert it into a nursery. The planning for our baby was so exciting, and it was a welcomed distraction for us, especially after the challenges we'd already faced. We pulled together in celebration, but sadly my health issues didn't stay away for long.

My sudden deafness could have been the result of either a very bad sinus infection, labyrinthitis, ototoxicity from too many toxic drugs, or an autoimmune inner ear disease, which occurs when your own body attacks itself. The reality was that no one knew, and no doctor was able to give me a definitive diagnosis, which was very frustrating to say the least. During my pregnancy, I started to develop large and painful ulcers in my throat. These ulcers resembled the appearance and texture of a canker sore, only they were bigger, and the ulcers carved out large holes in my throat and left scars in their wake. These ulcerations would only appear in the back of my throat, and would feel as painful, if not worse, than a very bad case of strep throat. I remember having had a few here and there when I was in my mid-thirties, but for some reason they were so few and far between that I assumed they were just canker sores.

When I was about four months pregnant, I remember the entire back of my throat was covered with what looked like a giant canker sore. It was so bad that I couldn't talk, or swallow food. This was life threatening to my unborn child; to be without food or water. I was admitted to the hospital, treated with pain meds, connected to IV fluids, and was forced to drink a heinous thick liquid, no matter how painful, every four hours. I remember the nurse coming in and watching me drink; holding tight to my hand as I struggled to swallow. It was a nutritional drink. The taste was okay, but the pain was not. The doctors had no idea what might be causing the massive ulcerations but decided that a smart course of action would be to administer steroid medication to see if it would have any effect.

It was from that point on that I developed a love-hate relationship with the steroid drug called Prednisone. It was a lifesaving drug for me whenever I had the massive, painful ulcerations. It was as if by magic that the sores melted away in the back of my throat just hours after administration. I was hours away from having a feeding tube inserted when they tried the steroids. The next day, I was able to swallow without pain, and within another three days, I was pain free and back home.

Sadly, I found myself in and out of the maternity ward at least five times over the course of my pregnancy as the ulcers went into overdrive. I felt happy on floor three as the nurses there dealt with good things, like new babies, and their days were filled with teaching new moms how to nurse their little ones. They were always welcoming, and I loved being there because despite hating the side effects from the steroid IV, I loved the fact that it wasn't long until I was pain free.

Being on and off steroids for the duration of my pregnancy made mood swings worse, but also further weakened my already weak immune system, which unknowingly set me up for a perfect storm.

It was a cold October morning at about 5 am when I woke to a gush of warm fluid running down my thighs. I ran to the toilet and was in shock as pink liquid poured out, and I was without any ability to control it. I called for Jesse and told him to call the hospital right away. The baby wasn't due for three more weeks, so I was terrified.

The date was October 27, 2016. We were told to come in as soon as possible, which we did without hesitation. They assured us over the phone that the pink fluid was nothing to be alarmed about and that amniotic fluid could be pink and not mean anything bad was happening per se. I was relieved and was choosing to remain calm and think positive as we made our way to the third floor. Once again, the nurses were welcoming and gave us a beautiful, quiet room to relax in while we began deciding how we were going to move forward. Jesse and I were excited, and in great spirits. The thought of meeting our child three weeks early was thrilling and we couldn't believe it was happening. We were laughing and joking with the nurses, and even posed for some playful photos of me pretending to push out a doll and the nurse catching it.

Eventually as the day wore on, playtime ended, and we needed to make a firm plan as to how the baby was going to get moving. Since my labor was not progressing at all, we all agreed to induce me to move things along. A decision was also made to administer some steroid medication because I had been on and off steroids throughout the pregnancy. The doctor felt it would be too taxing on my adrenal glands without that boost. I was happy with the plan, as it all seemed to make perfect sense.

Like clockwork, labour began and the excitement and anticipation were in overdrive. When the contractions started to become too painful to manage and the laughing gas was no longer making me laugh, I opted for the epidural. I am not one to be a hero and endure severe pain, and I had no desire to experience the "Ring of Fire." As the epidural set in, they decided that because

I was so comfortable and the baby was doing well, they could increase the induction meds and therefore speed up the process.

By this time, it was approximately 10 pm and things started to take a turn for the worse. It was so unexpected when the nurse couldn't get the concerned look off her face, and they demanded suddenly that I get on all fours. An epidural numbs the body from the waist down, so holding yourself up on all fours is not something you can just do. I struggled to do as I was told, though it wasn't easy, especially given that I also had a plethora of tubes and wires hanging off me.

The issue was that the speed with which we induced my labour began to stress out my little baby, causing the heart rate to drop rapidly, and at times become undetectable. It was so hard to believe, as just minutes earlier we had all been laughing, and the doctor on call, Dr. Love, was predicting the baby would be out soon. I had reached the 8.5 cm mark, and pushing, she said, would be imminent.

Now suddenly, we faced the reality that my baby could die if we didn't take immediate action. Jesse was thrown a pair of blue scrubs, and I was told that they were going to prep me for surgery. As Jesse was about to throw on the scrubs, the heart rate became too dangerously low to wait, and they called a CODE PINK. I was devastated. After all I had endured, why couldn't I just birth my baby? I had no time to lament as fifteen doctors and nurses ran to my bedside. They pushed my poor husband away and told him, "Sorry, there is no time." He looked on helplessly as they ripped all the monitor cables off of me and wheeled me away to the operating room at lightning speed.

I remember looking up and seeing a huge light in my face, and I felt myself lying on a frigid metal table. The room was cold and sterile. The nurse that was above me pressed a plastic oxygen mask over my mouth. She pushed it fast and hard, and I felt like

I couldn't breathe. She kept telling me to take deep breaths, but I struggled because it was squishing my nose and mouth. Soon I was gone.

The enormity of the situation was something that didn't hit us at the time, as it all happened too fast. My husband was laughing one minute, and the next was forced to stand alone in a room, not knowing if his wife or unborn child would be alive when he saw them next. I thought I was about to push, and the next minute I was unconscious and being cut open.

When I opened my eyes, I found myself in a dark area of the hospital. It was quiet, and there was very little light. I remember trembling, a known side effect of the sedation meds, and my teeth chattering. I tried to call for the only nurse I could see, whose back was to me, as she seemed to be feverishly typing something into a computer. She came straight over.

I asked where I was, and she said I was in the recovery room and that my baby was doing well and was upstairs with my husband. I was in shock, and all I wanted was to see my baby. I asked what I had, and she told me I'd had a boy. *I had a boy!* My spine tingled, and my entire body was covered in goosebumps as she told me about my healthy five-pound son. We had our 'Jack'. I couldn't believe it.

It seemed like it took an eternity for me to stabilize so that I could finally be wheeled up to the maternity ward where I found my husband slumped over in a pull-out armchair bed. He was barely visible as the blanket covered large sections of his exhausted face. He woke suddenly as they wheeled me in, and he greeted me with as much enthusiasm as possible. I asked to see my son, but he told me that despite having held him right after the birth, they took him away to test him and ensure that he was thriving.

Just as we finished recounting what had happened, a beautiful, older, blonde nurse with a perfect pixie cut, came in pushing a clear plastic bassinet. Inside was my beautiful son. His eyes struggled to see, and his head was covered with a navy-blue hand-made toque, lovingly created by hospital volunteers. He was wrapped tightly in a white and blue blanket and looked angelic.

"Meet your son." said the nurse as she wheeled him to my bedside. The tears flowed as I got to meet Jack. I felt a bit of emptiness inside, as his soul no longer resided within me. I found I had that same temporary void as when I gave birth to my daughter Rachael, twelve years earlier. I instantly fell in love with beautiful Jack, and the harrowing way he entered the world was soon forgotten as we spent the late hours of the night gazing at our baby son.

# CHAPTER TEN

# What's Happening to Me?

The morning after Jack was born, the nurse entered my room and told me I needed to go have a CT scan of my abdomen. I was, understandably, quite surprised when she told me that the doctor thought she may have nicked my ureter during the operation. So, there I sat in total panic just hours after my son's birth, wondering what kind of ramifications there might be should she in fact have cut my ureter.

They wheeled me down shortly after, and it thankfully wasn't long before they told me that I was okay and that everything looked as it should. Just before leaving the hospital, I went to the bathroom and noticed there was some blood in the bowl. I disregarded it, thinking that it was likely due to being constipated and perhaps straining.

I was discharged, and as I was walking out, I told the nurses that I felt extremely weak and dizzy. They told me it was probably psychological because apparently a nurse had told me my hemoglobin was quite low. I didn't remember being told that, and I brushed off her remark and went home.

Two days later, I woke up fatigued and weak, and I felt helpless as I tried to change the baby. I really struggled with severe guilt because for years my husband had to care for me in so many ways; with my deafness and having to relearn to walk, that I really wanted to take the burden of the baby off his hands. He did, after all, have the business to maintain, and yet he was getting up five times a night to bring me the crying baby to feed.

I just couldn't manage at all, and I also couldn't pretend that

everything was fine. I nearly collapsed. I also had the worst stabbing pains in my head. I looked in the mirror and I saw a ghost.
I looked dead. I told him to call 911.

Within an hour I was in the ICU (unbeknownst to me) and was
connected to hundreds of lines. A nice Asian doctor approached
me as calm as a cucumber, while my husband looked on with
worry, and my son lay sleeping angelically a few feet away.
"Have you ever had a blood transfusion?" she asked.

I had no idea why she was asking, but she informed that I was
about to have my first one. Apparently, my hemoglobin count
was extremely low. It was a fifty, and they transfuse at seventy or
less. That certainly explained why I was so pale. Without hesitation, I signed the risk-consent form, and prayed for the blood to
hurry because I was feeling extremely weak and unwell. The
doctor assured me that would be rectified after I got the blood.

Hours later I was finished, and I was free to go home. It was
hard for us to understand where all that blood had gone. I think
because I'd had a C-section earlier, they assumed that the blood
loss was related, and they sent me on my way.

As I settled back in at home with the baby, I remember how
hard it was and how bad I felt, and I just couldn't explain it. I
felt weak, and I started to develop stomach pain on the left side
of my abdomen. I also had a constant low-grade fever and night
sweats, in addition to no appetite whatsoever. Again, I went to
the emergency room asking for help, and the ER doctor said he
was worried that I'd had complications from the C-section, and
perhaps that was why I was having the issues. He reluctantly
suggested a CT scan. I say reluctantly because he knew I'd just
had one a few weeks prior, after the birth. The area that I was
pressing on was the spleen area, so he drew some blood and
went ahead with the CT. When he came back, he said he saw a
tiny infarction – an area of dead tissue – on my spleen. He said

that many people can have it. He told me if you scan ten people, one could have it, and it doesn't mean anything sinister, but it could also have just happened and cause pain. They couldn't find anything else wrong, and I was sent home again.

I still felt awful. As the days turned into months, I visited the ER many more times. I had a host of symptoms, including blood in my urine and what felt like kidney pain and even chest pain. I was scanned repeatedly, and went into a machine that suggested I could have had a clot in my lungs and was put on blood thinners. I also found out I had sponge kidney, which I was apparently born with. It just meant that I was more likely to produce kidney stones. They found that I had at least a dozen tiny stones in each kidney, which they said should cause no pain. I was at a loss as to what to do or where to turn as I was tested and scanned, and nothing concrete ever showed up.

My lowest point was that Christmas, when Jack was two months old, and I was to fly to my favorite place in Dundas, Ontario to see Jesse's grandmother. During the flight, I remember feeling that tight, painful feeling in my chest and worrying about whether I had a blood clot. I also had what I thought was pain from kidney stones, and I had a constant, low-grade fever, and severe pain when I lay on my back in bed. I was researching how to get rid of kidney stones, thinking they were causing me all of these problems. I began consuming large quantities of olive oil and lemon juice because I read that would clean out the kidneys.

One night when things became unbearable for me, I had to have Jesse take me to the ER in the middle of the night. I began to think that I would be sick forever, and that soon my husband would surely tire of me, and everyone, including myself, would think I was starting to go crazy. I knew deep down that I wasn't. I tried to overlook the judgment I knew some people were making, and somehow, I held faith that all would be ok.

# CHAPTER ELEVEN

# More Testing

The concerned ER doctor came in and assessed me. He told me that he was worried that I might have a blood clot in my lung and thought we needed to rule that out. He also wanted to do a CT of my abdomen because of what felt like kidney pain. I just remember putting my head in my hands and crying, realizing that I would once again have no choice but to have another two CT scans done; toxic red dye injected into my already stressed kidneys, and then likely be told they had no answers.

The worry was that if I had a clot and left it, then it could be fatal. I asked to have a D-dimer blood test first. At this point, I was a medical Googler, and had become savvy about many of the tests and possible outcomes. I knew that if my D-dimer test read negative, then I would have no clot, but if it was positive, I could have one. There was a chance that it could show a false positive because a nursing or pregnant woman can show that result. The doctor felt it would likely come back positive and even though I agreed, in the event it was negative, I wanted the chance to save my body from further radiation damage.

Once again, I was given an IV of Gravol (anti-nausea), and morphine, as well as an Advil equivalent. The pain was then manageable, and I lay anxious but pain-free. The hours passed slowly, and the agony of being away from my infant son for the first time was intense to say the least. I was worried about how they would manage without me, but thankfully, he was drinking formula rather than breast milk because I often had drugs in my system and had to pump and toss the milk for his safety.

When the doctor returned, he didn't bring good news. He said the dimer test was positive, and I would need to go ahead with the two scans. I took a deep breath and went for it. It was such a lonely and difficult experience for me because not only did I fear for my life at that point, but I feared I wouldn't be able to care for my son, and that I would also be a burden to my husband.

When the doctor came back, he told me I had no clot and my CT only showed sponge kidney and many little stones, which he felt should not be causing any pain. We left again without any answers.

Over several days the pain seemed to lessen, and I managed what felt like a low-grade fever with Tylenol, and I sat down each time the abdominal pains resurfaced. I started to resign myself to the fact that these mysterious symptoms, however painful, clearly could not be life threatening, as I had been scanned multiple times and nothing was found.

We flew back to Vancouver in early January, and I remember feeling weak and tired every day. I felt so helpless because I had challenges with my hearing, and on top of that, I was becoming an invalid-of-sorts that needed my family to check in on me at regular intervals to ensure I was able to manage.

The mouth ulcerations, which I kept getting with increasing frequency, made eating nearly impossible, and with the nausea and stomach pains, I found my weight started to plummet. I was down to 120 pounds after having been 186 pounds at the time I had Jack. That was a significant weight loss. We had been to every oral surgeon, ENT, and rheumatologist in Vancouver by this point, and visited the ER at least ten times. The consensus by most doctors was that I had some kind of autoimmune process going on, but until more ugly symptoms appeared, it would be unlikely that they could pinpoint the diagnosis and treat me.

One morning I went to the washroom, looked down, and saw a lot of blood. I called for Jesse. I remember my legs feeling weak as fear took over. I drove myself to the ER and told the nurse that I had passed blood, and they attended to me rather quickly. I was given a bed, and within an hour I had gone to the toilet at least five more times, passing more and more blood. Suddenly, I was no longer able to walk. My legs felt too weak and I collapsed in the hallway. The nurses yelled at me, telling me I was pretending, and to just stand up. I tried to tell them what I was feeling, but by this point many of the nurses thought I was crazy because they had seen me so often. With reluctance, the nurses helped me back to my bed and connected me to the monitors. The ER doctor emerged, and I was connected to the heart rate and blood pressure monitors. My blood pressure dropped, and my pulse went sky high. I became very pale. I told the nurse I was losing feeling in my hands and feet, and she just brushed me off and said I was having a panic attack. I asked for a bedside toilet, which they brought, but after making it on there only once, I became bedridden and could no longer stand. I called for the nurse and she came, holding a tray for me to pass huge quantities of blood, which at this point wouldn't stop pouring out of my rectum. I thought I was going to die.

I remember my mom walking in around the time when the nurse had to hold the tray there, and she turned sheet white when she saw my condition. She was in total shock. The ER doctor came in regularly and said he was keeping an eye on my hemoglobin, which at first he said was still okay; it was at ninety. Every hour they tested me and each time they reported it was ten points lower. It was eighty, then seventy, then sixty, then at fifty they finally said they would get me some blood. They ran tests while I was lying there, and the doctor told me that I had caught C. Difficile. C. Difficile, or Clostridioides difficile, is a species of gram-positive spore-forming bacterium which infects humans and other animals. Usually the elderly and those with very weak immune systems are vulnerable.

The symptoms of "C. diff." are fever, stomach pains, dehydration, nausea, loss of appetite, and diarrhea. *Could this be what had caused my life to be such hell since my son's birth?* Hospitals are a prime place for this nasty toxin to lurk, and being that I was cut open recently and was on steroid drugs, which weaken your immune system, it seemed like that could have created the perfect storm for me.

The blood seemed to take forever to arrive. I was getting weaker and weaker, and I was feeling scared because I could no longer feel my limbs. I told the doctor that my heart rate was now 225 and my pulse was 80/40 and he told me again that I was just anxious, and they handed me an Ativan to quiet me down. The blood was taking so long because they waited till my hemoglobin hit fifty before ordering, and because this was my second transfusion, I had built up antibodies and they needed to source the blood from a different hospital.

I arrived at the ER at 9 am, and did not receive the blood transfusion until 11 pm. The doctor that was taking care of me had also treated me a few weeks before when I had come in because of blood in my urine. At that time, he diagnosed me with a bladder infection and prescribed antibiotics, which killed all my good gut bacteria, and likely enabled the C. diff. toxin to take over completely, causing the bloody stool. He and I didn't see eye to eye that time when I came in. I was so unwell, and I had begged him to let me stay when I had the supposed bladder infection, but he insisted I go home and return to visit the infectious disease doctor as an outpatient instead.

This time I was admitted, and was to be monitored. I was placed in a room on the sixth floor and was assigned an internal medicine doctor to ensure I was properly treated to get the serious infection under control. Unfortunately, he felt another CT scan was important to look at my intestinal tract, and make sure there was nothing else that could have caused so much bleeding. I was put on a drug called Vancomycin, which, when taken correctly, is effective at eradicating the C. diff.

I was also told I was going to need a colonoscopy. I was terrified. I had to drink an awful liquid which tasted horrible, and I was already so nauseated. On top of that, it caused me to have intense diarrhea, and I was afraid I would start bleeding again. All of this, plus another CT scan! It was a nightmare.

I braved whatever I had to in order to hopefully find an end to my pain and suffering, and get back to my baby. The doctor came back, read the results of my CT, and told me that both of my kidneys had infarcted. I had no idea what that meant. He said that a small area of each kidney had died, and it looked like either a small clot on each side or an area of dead tissue from getting no blood supply.

I told him that I'd had a scan a week prior in Ontario and there was no such infarction. I asked him if it was possible that this happened because they left me so long without blood and if the lack of fluid and blood going through the kidneys could have caused this. He, of course, didn't want to implicate the doctors and suggested that it was very unlikely, but in my mind, I will always feel that they waited too long to give me blood, and as a result my kidneys paid the price. The doctor felt that he needed to rule out a heart problem because sometimes the heart can do something funky and throw out clots into your body. Next, I had to have a comprehensive heart test, but that showed nothing. I waited for the results of the colonoscopy and it showed an area of colon that was irritated. He likened it to the appearance of a skinned knee. He said it looked consistent with the kind of irritation that C. Diff. would cause. The doctors did not feel the way I bled was consistent with having C. Diff. though. He couldn't directly see a cause for the massive amount of blood loss.

After I was able to pass a semi-solid and blood-free stool, and keep some food in my stomach, I was released and sent back home. I was terrified, yet somewhat hopeful that we had figured out what may have caused the horrible symptoms I had been having. Perhaps the infection was the reason for the stomach pains and low-grade fever, and the bladder infection was the cause of the pains in my kidneys and the blood in my urine. *Maybe I had those infections all along and it was due to being cut open in a hospital and on steroids that made me a candidate for all these issues.* All I hoped was that my luck would change, and that I could finally try to be a mother to my newborn son.

# CHAPTER TWELVE

# Finally, an Answer?

After returning home, I had many months of discomfort as I fought to kill the C. Difficile infection. I took the antibiotics four times a day, which made me feel nauseated and gave me stomach cramps. After some time passed, I began to feel a bit better and the fever went away. I was still extremely pale, and my iron and hemoglobin remained very low. I always felt weak, and my internist began sending me to the hospital to have IV iron infusions every two weeks.

My heart rate was always at 90, which for me was abnormal as I used to always sit at around 66 beats. When you become sick for a long period of time, you start monitoring and researching everything and trying to help yourself because you feel like no one else is finding out what's wrong with you.

At this point in time, the biggest source of pain and anguish came from my mouth ulcerations, which seemed relentless. These things would take over my entire throat making it impossible to eat or drink without screaming. I found myself in and out of the hospital almost daily getting IV steroids, Gravol, and morphine just to calm them down so I could swallow. My face and body would swell. I would feel like I was dying after five days on the high doses and then stopping treatment. It was a roller coaster. When I was getting the steroids, my mouth would heal and I could eat, but then I would lay awake all night, wired, and my moods would swing wildly. It was so unpleasant, but it became my life.

Jesse and I often talked about visiting one of the top medical facilities in the world to seek answers. The Mayo Clinic has several facilities worldwide, but we chose to go to the clinic in Minnesota. We heard that the costs of treatment in the United States were astronomical, and we prepared ourselves accordingly.

While we began making all the arrangements, we mentioned it to our doctors, and it was suggested to us that we apply to BC Medical as they have a program to help with the costs. If you have exhausted all your options within Canada, and have not been able to find a cure, then they would consider coverage on a case-by-case basis. We began filling out the paperwork, making our case, and getting many of our doctors to assist and sign off. The rationale was essentially a trade-off for them: since we were in the ER over a dozen times that year with no treatment solution, rather than continuing to visit the local hospital at however many thousands of dollars per visit, financially it made more sense for them to send us to these specialists at the Mayo.

The day we received the formal letter informing us that we were approved to go and that all our out-of-province medical costs would be reimbursed was an amazing day to say the least. We were going regardless, and this made it much less taxing on our family. They told us the costs could easily total $30,000 – and that was just for a short five-day investigative visit. We jumped up and down as if we had won the lottery.

It was September 2017. Jack was eleven months old, and we packed him up and made the journey to cold Minnesota. Arriving at the Mayo Clinic felt like what Dorothy saw when she arrived in Oz. The towers were grand, and the list of doctors and specialists seemed endless as you stood in the lobby. The bustle inside was palpable. You could feel the desperation in the air from so many hopeful people who had flown in from all over the world, searching for answers.

It was still crazy to us that this was our new reality. We had one year of near bliss in our relationship, and since that time we had endured one health challenge after another. We were finding our new normal, and this was it. Our family holidays were to the world-renowned Mayo Clinic.

We settled into our hotel and made it as fun as we could. We were given our schedule of appointments upon check in, and told how everything worked. You would go to the payment desk and make your massive deposit, earning you credits to go see your $1,000+/hour doctors. There was a north tower and a south tower, and each floor had its own specialty, like Ears, Nose, and Throat, or Gastroenterology. There are two towers: the Mayo Building and the newer Gonda Building. There was an intricate underground system of walkways spanning several city blocks that would lead us directly from our hotel room to our various appointments within the 'clinic.' It was an incredible network that allowed patients to make it to their appointments without needing to venture out in the cold Minnesota weather. This very well thought out underground system connected the clinic to malls, hotels and food courts. We had everything we needed right underneath our hotel.

I would leave the room, pass the shops, grab my coffee and muffin, and in just six short minutes of navigating the underground tunnels, I was right in the heart of the Mayo clinic.

My first appointment was with an internal medicine doctor who was in charge of my case while I was there. He reviewed my files before our meeting, and was fascinated by my crazy history. He, like most doctors, was baffled by my case. Sudden deafness, massive GI bleed, blood transfusions, C. difficile and crippling throat ulcerations. They all felt that it was an autoimmune disease but couldn't tie everything together. Many thought I had Behcet's disease, which is characterized by ulcerations in the mouth but also had many other symptoms, which I thankfully never had, like red, painful, weeping eyes, and skin symptoms like rashes and sores. I was personally convinced that I did not have Bechet's disease, because the sores were in my throat rather than in my mouth. To me it made a difference, as all the photos I saw did not resemble what I had.

I listened as the doctor described what my week would look like, and how the system would work. He told me that he would review all of the doctors' comments and would give me a summary at the end. I could hardly wait. We were so excited, and felt hope for the first time in a long time. We thought maybe we would finally be free of my mysterious health issues.

After regularly being poked, scanned, x-rayed, and examined, our week was complete. We waited in many waiting rooms all over the clinic, and met a handful of interesting people also with intricate medical histories such as mine. Jack made quite a few friends during our short stay. We sat with anticipation as we waited for our final meeting with the Internal Medicine doctor. He told us that the conclusion was that I likely had Bechet's or a similar autoimmune disease that would be helped by taking a biologic drug called Humira or something similar.

It was a 'guess' again, and not a certain diagnosis. It was also a huge disappointment. As you can imagine, taking a powerful injected drug every month, which itself has a whole host of possible side effects, seemed daunting; especially if you were not sure whether it was the correct diagnosis.

We flew home defeated. The only thing we held onto was that all the doctors said that I had been examined so thoroughly over the past year, that they knew that whatever was going on was not life threatening, just extremely uncomfortable.

## CHAPTER THIRTEEN

# I Want to Die

As fall passed into winter, we celebrated a much better Christmas than the year before. Jack was now one, and he could open a gift and express excitement while doing so. My life at this point was better because the intense pain in my stomach was not as bad, and the throat sores would come and go with a bit less frequency.

I was trying so hard to be the Monique that I remembered, but it was very hard to find my footing. People that didn't know me didn't treat me differently because I looked the same, but many of the people that I thought were my friends were not there for me during my hardest times. It completely changed the way that I viewed my world.

While I lay in the hospital dozens of times, the only constants were my husband, Jesse, who came every day without fail, my daughter whenever she could, and my mother. My mom brought me food and drinks, and my husband raced around trying to maintain our real estate business while carrying our infant son on his arm. He brought me magazines and flowers, and he would sit at my bedside and offer the most encouraging words.

At times I was so sick that I wanted to die. One time when I was admitted to Vancouver General Hospital, I was assigned a team of internal medicine doctors, and they made it their mission to help me find answers. Like many doctors before them, they were baffled by my case and felt sorry for me, as I had a young baby, and they wanted to help. They scanned my abdomen and one morning an intern that was part of my team came in and told me that I had fifteen clots on my spleen! Fifteen! I was in absolute shock. They said they wanted to put me on 1000 mg of steroids per day for three days, otherwise I might die. They were convinced that my heart was throwing out clots again and that maybe that was why my kidneys had those infarctions, and maybe that's why I went deaf. I felt that it was all crazy, but I had to listen. I was told shortly thereafter that she was *so sorry* because she had misread the image, and the markings she thought were clots were in fact dots on the computer screen! Just another day in the life.

If that wasn't bad enough, during the same visit, I was told that my heart test had shown that I had a hole in my heart. This hole, they said, was good news because it could explain some of my issues and was easily fixable, with a small surgery where they would place mesh over the hole. They told me they had to operate immediately. As I was wheeled down to have the procedure, I was understandably terrified. While laying in the room waiting for the doctor to begin, he came in and told me he was very sorry, but that my heart was perfectly fine and that someone had misread the tests! Again!

Could any of it be real? At this point I thought the hospital might be causing me more harm than good. It seemed that aside from Jesse and my mom, I had very little support, and it left me lonely. I was constantly consumed with guilt because I felt disconnected from my son. The bond I shared with my baby was disrupted by my constant absence. My friends were often absent, and my husband's family must have thought poor Jesse was so taxed because he married a woman who was not only deaf, but who was so frequently in the hospital. I was judged by the nurses, and my once positive spirit was becoming negative and dark. I sometimes thought that I wished I would die. I literally only lived to see Jesse, my mom, Rachael, and Jack.

Those were the darkest times of my life, and it's hard for anyone to imagine the world I was living in. From the outside, people assumed we had it all perfect. The one thing we did have, which is perfect, was love. My husband meant his vows; he did love me unconditionally, and that was all I had ever wished to find, and I had it.

His love was enough. I didn't need anyone else. I knew that I had to dig deeper, pull myself out of the self-pity I had sunk into, and rise back up. I wanted to be there to support Jesse, Jack, and Rachael at all costs.

I decided to fight the pain and weakness, and learn to accept it. I gave up hope that I would ever find a cure, or even a cause. I was tired of hospitals, and done with nurses talking down to me. I turned a corner mentally, which was half the battle. I learned that life was a gift and there are always people that have it much worse. I could talk, and I could feel, and I had love, and that was all I needed.

# CHAPTER FOURTEEN

# Out of Options

In January 2018 we had an unfortunate start to the year, as Jesse lost his father. It was a challenging time for us, as his death was sudden and totally unexpected. When Jesse's dad got sick, we sat by his bedside every day in the ICU. I felt closely connected to him, even in his unconscious state, because I knew in my heart what it felt like to be lying there at the mercy of your illness.

I did all that I could to show support to my husband and give back to him some of what he had given to me. He was brave. After his father passed, we held a service. Jesse's celebration of life speech was beautiful, and when he couldn't manage to finish it, I stood up and helped him.

The morning of the funeral, I remember thinking I might not make it. I woke up again with really bad pains in my stomach. I just couldn't believe the timing. I fought so hard that day because I knew my husband needed me more than ever. I had a fever and pain, but I just refused to go to the hospital again. A few weeks later, we had to go in because I had a bad chest cough, and we were told I had pneumonia. I was terrified of being on antibiotics because after I had C. difficile a few months before, I'd had a relapse. I was afraid that the antibiotics would surely wipe out all the good bacteria I had and cause me to relapse again. I was in tears when the doctor told me the news. Again, I had no choice but to try and cure the pneumonia, and take the drugs.

Three days later I was no better, and Jesse was out. I decided to take a cab to Lions Gate Hospital, which I had never done, because Jesse had inadvertently taken my car keys. When I arrived in the ER, my plan was to just pop in, see a doctor, and get a new prescription. The nurses knew me well, and told me that they were sorry, but they had an unusually long wait time in the ER of more than nine hours.

Then I made the decision to take another cab over two bridges to Vancouver General Hospital. It was a short wait to see the doctor. He examined me briefly, and was about to send me home with a prescription.

I was having a hard time sitting in the waiting room for some reason, as I felt very weak and dizzy. Suddenly the doctor came back to get me, and said that he would feel better taking an x-ray and running a few tests before sending me home. I'm not sure what changed his mind. I was given some fluids through the IV. I had a mild fever and my pulse was fast. The nurse was not overly concerned as I did have pneumonia. The doctor had come to send me home, and I was about to get into the cab, when a new female doctor that had just come on shift ran out to grab me. She informed me that she wanted me to come back because the nurse had told her about my high pulse rate. She told me she'd feel better if she kept me overnight to monitor me. I was so surprised but grateful, as I felt extremely weak. At that time, I had an abscess on my leg that was quite painful and would not heal. It had been caused by a metal post from a flowerpot wheelbarrow that had stabbed me in the shin a few weeks earlier. I also had a large mouth ulcer, stomach pain, and pneumonia. I wanted relief from one or more of my issues.

She gave me a bed with a curtain in the ER, and told me my magnesium was low and she wanted to give me an IV. I went to sleep and woke the next morning being told that I was going to be admitted, moved upstairs, and assigned a team of doctors. I was so happy, because I needed some help.

Just as I settled into my room, I had an urgent need to go to the washroom. I sat in disbelief as blood began to pour out of my rectum again. I ran for help, calling the nurse and telling them frantically that I had about an hour, and if they didn't get blood I would likely die. The nurse listened and sent a special doctor to my bedside. They ordered blood and promised to check my hemoglobin. I told them that I had bled before, that it happens fast, and that they would need to cross match.

They listened and took no chances. Again, I could manage walking to the toilet once or twice, and then I needed a bedside toilet. Within forty minutes, I could no longer sit up, let alone stand. I did manage a quick text telling Jesse what was happening, but I told him to stay home with the kids. It was a long drive, and I thought I was in good hands.

After an hour, my vital signs were low, and I had ten nurses and two doctors at my bedside. I had four IVs connected in different locations on my body as different fluids went in to try to sustain me until the blood arrived. The nurses were terrified and devastated, as they knew my story, and knew I had a young son.

I remember them holding my hands as I faded in and out of consciousness. I was not afraid to die. I was sad that I might not see Jesse and my children again, but I was tired of fighting. I felt at peace. I knew that I had ended up in that ER, on that day, for a reason. It occurred to me that I had come to change medications, and had I been anywhere else, I would most certainly have died.

It was a race against the clock as my vitals kept dropping fast. The blood was still pouring out of me as I lay on my side. I could not feel my arms or legs, and I felt that I'd soon lose my brain, too. They stabbed a long needle through the main vein in my wrist to test my carbon dioxide levels.

The doctor was holding my hand, too, and offering me encouraging words. He kept running into the halls to look for the blood. It was not there. I was being pumped full of fluids and, in the last five minutes, I had a second wind. It was like a miracle. I remember telling God in my mind that I knew it was fate that I was there when the bleeding started. It was only one hour later, and I was almost dead. Had I been at home when it started, I wouldn't have had time, and I would have died. I told God that I knew He would either take me then, or the bleeding would result in my being cured. After those words, I was temporarily, as if by magic, more conscious, and my mind was more alert.

Moments later, the blood bags showed up, and I knew then that my cure was coming. I knew that I would not have been put through that massive bleed and nearly die for nothing.

# CHAPTER FIFTEEN

# A Diagnosis

Shortly after I received the blood, I was feeling worlds better, but I knew that I needed to strike while the iron was hot. If there's one thing I learned from the process, it's that you need to be your own advocate. You can't sit back and assume the healthcare system will find your cure or not forget about you. The system is taxed, and the nurses and doctors are overworked. It is up to you to self-advocate.

I asked for the doctor in charge of me to create a plan for me. Despite having had three colonoscopies by that point, I demanded an immediate one to see if they could find the cause of this bleed. I felt in my gut that this bleed and its cause would result in my cure. The doctor that was assigned to me was reluctant, which was shocking. He had apparently reviewed my history and seen that I had contracted C. difficile twice and felt certain that that was what I must have again. He insisted I take the C. diff drugs, despite my insistence that I did not have it. The quarantine signs went up outside my room, and I was forced to wait three days for the test results to come back. I was dumbfounded.

At first he promised a colonoscopy, but then retracted that decision when he read my file. I talked at length with him, pleading with him and explaining that I did not have any of the C. diff symptoms.

After three days the results came back, and I was not sick with the C. diff toxin as I had repeatedly insisted. The doctor agreed to do a mini colonoscopy to view the area that previously looked skinned to see if it had gotten worse, and could have caused the bleed. They also did a topographical CT scan to see if there was anything obviously visible in my small and large bowel. I fully expected to be choking back the horrible bowel prep drinks before my colonoscopy, but without warning they picked me up and wheeled me down for the procedure.

When I arrived, the nurse asked me if I had done the bowel prep and I said no, and she said it was okay because they would give me a mini enema. That did not happen, and the doctor went in with the scope. I was watching the monitor, and could not see the walls of my colon at all. I was not prepped, so how they expected to examine me was beyond me. I was wheeled back up to my room, and that was it.

I immediately contacted my internist, Dr. Kevin McLeod, who had been my guardian angel and rock throughout the painful journey. He wanted nothing more than to help me and find out what was happening to me. He helped rush an appointment with a well-known gastroenterologist, Dr. Gregory Monkewich, who sat with me almost immediately. We were going to do a camera study where I was to swallow a small pill-sized camera that would take thirty thousand snapshots of the small bowel on the way down. We thought the answers would lie somewhere in the photos. This time we decided to finally do that study, but first we thought it best if we prepped my bowels properly, and went into the large intestine first with a regular colonoscopy. I was prepped and on the table in early March 2018.

I was so excited for this colonoscopy that I think the nurses were taken aback. For some reason, I just felt that this time we'd finally find my answer. As I drifted in and out of sleep, I remember opening my eyes for a brief moment and fixating on a small white patch that resembled the ulcers that I so often saw in my throat. Immediately, I called out to the doctor. I asked loudly what it was and his reply, which I will never forget, was, "I think I found your problem."

Tears of joy streamed down my face and the emotion that took over my body was indescribable. I was filled with hope and wonder as I waited for him in recovery to deliver his diagnosis.

As I slowly became fully alert in the recovery area, the nurse brought me the usual cookies and overly sweet juice. Never did either taste better. I was chatting away to anyone who would listen. I think it was nervous chatter, which was helpful during the agonizing wait.

The doctor approached, and I think I accosted him. I know my arms flung up and I tried to hug him, but he stepped back and offered his hand. He is not a hugger. He began by telling me that I had Crohn's disease, which baffled my mind. He said that he saw forty deep ulcers in a small section of my colon, and that some were so deep that he felt it likely burst a vessel, which caused the bleed. I was shocked, mainly because other than the two massive bleeds, I didn't really have bowel symptoms, or maybe I did but I thought that was C. difficile.

He explained that ulcers can form anywhere in the intestinal tract, which starts in your mouth. That was fascinating to me. That explained the fact that the ulcers were always in the back of my throat and not in my mouth per se. It explained the fevers and the occasional cramping pains. It explained my low iron and my low hemoglobin. It explained why I was always fighting and getting sick. I was caught in a cycle that now could finally end.

He told me that I would be starting an IV medication called Infliximab or Remicade, and that it would put me into remission. He said that I may never have symptoms again. I was over the moon. I could hardly contain myself as I tried to tell everyone in my family at the same time. I could barely get the words out to Jesse. I knew this meant we, and especially he, would get a chance at a normal life again. I knew it meant my son would have his mom, and my daughter and I would make up for lost time.

I knew the day that I nearly died, that nothing in my life was accidental. I knew my pain would end one way or another, and I made peace with whatever the outcome might be.

# CHAPTER SIXTEEN

# Peace

Knowing you will be cured is one thing, but learning and researching your cure and its possible effects is another. As I have stated, I am a medical Googler. The first thing I did is Google Remicade and its possible side effects. To say they are scary is an understatement. Possible liver failure, allergic life-threatening reactions, increased risk of developing tuberculosis, and so many other things pop up. I knew I had no choice and that I had to be brave, but the day I drove out to get the first dose, my legs were so weak from fear I could barely exit the car.

I had a mouth ulcer the day of my first dose, and I was in tears as I recounted to the nurse what had brought me to her that day. I don't think I could talk about my journey much without bursting into tears. When you are going through it, you are in a constant state of fight or flight, but when you stop fighting you feel an overwhelming flood of emotions.

As she calmly walked me through what would happen, I settled into my recliner and grabbed some magazines as a welcome distraction. My mom and Jesse had made the trip with me, but they were not allowed to sit with me during treatment, so it would be up to me to be brave. I held the bag of meds in my hand and closed my eyes. I visualized it pouring into my veins like gold and only doing good things to me. Someone suggested I try to visualize the meds healing me, so I did. As she set up the IV, she began the drip slowly to ensure she could catch any allergic reaction. The IV went faster and faster, and four hours later, I was still breathing as I walked away from the clinic.

For the first twenty-four hours I was fearful and almost waiting for a bad reaction. I did feel headaches during the initial treatment, and I felt tired post-infusion, but I watched as the mouth ulcer I had just melted away. It was my miracle. I was grateful to the doctors who heard me, and to the nurses who were kind and to my family, and who held me up during the days I didn't see a point in carrying on.

For the next six months, into the fall of 2018, I was able to enjoy my life again in ways I had all but forgotten. I could swallow without pain. Imagine if every time you swallowed you screamed like strep throat for years, and then suddenly one day that pain was gone. People take swallowing for granted, but I never will.

My blood work normalized as well, and I watched as my iron went from a 2 to a 15.5! My hemoglobin, which was a seventy, went to one hundred thirty-five, and all the other irregular blood work normalized. My kidneys, sadly, never regained their normal numbers, but in my lifetime, they should carry me through just fine. They are functioning at about ninety percent, and the two infarctions are what I affectionately refer to as my battle scars.

From 1973 to 2014, I took my great health for granted. Between 2014 and 2018, I went deaf suddenly, I relearned to walk, and I lost my balance organs permanently. I had cochlear implant surgery and relearned to hear. I had Bell's palsy and half my face was paralyzed. I caught C. diff, twice. I nearly bled to death on two occasions. I had six blood transfusions. I was diagnosed with sponge kidney and had stone removal surgery. I had five colonoscopies, a kidney and bladder infection, and both my kidneys infarcted. I had thirteen CT scans, a kidney biopsy, a spinal tap, several brain scans, more than thirty ulcerations in my throat, and I swallowed my uvula for breakfast after it became so ulcerated that it fell off. I had a beautiful son in the middle of all of that, and his birth resulted from an emergency C-section. It has been a long four years and I will never be unscathed from its aftermath.

I now am a deaf woman who has Crohn's disease, but I am still Monique. The challenge now becomes learning how I proceed. Do I define myself by the illness that I have, or do I reinvent myself and learn a new normal? Jesse and I have had many new normal to learn along the many unfamiliar roads we were forced down, and it is not easy, but it is the only way forward.

# Chapter Seventeen

# Healing

The process of healing from something like this is very hard to describe. On the one hand, you are healed on a physical level, but the emotional healing takes months, even years, and in some cases can leave permanent scars.

My dream all my life was to somehow help and inspire others in some way, but I never knew how. I had no idea that posting on social media, just small fractions of what I was going through, could help me achieve just that. I found comfort in my cyber friends and found that I looked forward daily to reading their words of encouragement. Those thoughtful and heartfelt words actually helped me push through some of my darkest days. I was told that I was courageous and strong in times when I felt weak and full of despair. I was told I was an inspiration. Me? Who would have thought that I was fulfilling a lifelong dream by lying in my hospital bed and sharing my trials and tribulations? I guess I was getting what I wished for and that somehow, maybe, there was a message in all of the pain. Perhaps that I was strong and really was brave, and that I truly was inspiring to some people.

I learned through this journey that you really don't know who your friends are until your darkest hours come and go. You really are your own best friend in dire times, and I quickly learned to look inward for guidance from my own inner voice. I found when I was quiet, I was clearly guided as to how to best proceed. I learned that you can't have expectations for anyone, as they will only lead to frustration and disappointment. I received no support from the people I most expected it from, but I also received support from some amazing people who stepped up and will now be lifelong friends. There is always a silver lining.

After all was said and done, I felt like I had been chewed up and spit out. Despite feeling better than ever, I was still hard of hearing, which meant that I needed to find a way to reinvent myself. I knew I still loved selling, and I wanted to maintain my real estate business with Jesse, but many things I used to take for granted, like calling ten clients a day to see how they were and following up on leads on the phone, were no longer possible. I can hear on the phone, for the most part, when I hear voices that I am used to, but sometimes my brain can mishear a word. That doesn't work well if you're negotiating a real estate deal. That meant relying and depending on Jesse to help me fill in the gaps where I was unable to. It is still difficult for me, someone who spent forty-one years as a strong, fiercely independent person, to take a back seat and allow someone else to take the reins. That aspect of my life was needed in order for me to grow on a spiritual level.

I think I always felt the need to be in control and drive the bus. Learning to let go and allow someone else to take over for me has been one of my life's biggest challenges. It can result in my ego being bruised, feeling 'less than,' vulnerable, unworthy and just plain small. I was no longer greeting clients at open houses with enthusiasm and confidence. I now stand behind Jesse, who has taken over, and I jump in when I can and assist. It is a very different dynamic and it takes a lot of getting used to.

The way forward was to focus on what I can still do. I could talk face to face and bring in business for Williamson Real Estate. I'll never forget the first healthy feeling summer; Jack and I handed out gift cards for ice cream to try and drive traffic to one of our listings. I could talk and listen in person and so, too, could I sell and drive traffic. I became the PR person for the business, and I still did open houses, but not alone. I can door knock, and I can help advise Jesse when he needs it. I am also responsible for the lives of my two children, which are more valuable and important than anything. I wanted to slow down and focus on them, and simply learn to be present in their lives. I found that even that was something I had taken for granted.

I receive emails and texts from people who have hearing issues come up. These are people that I barely know that have contacted me, frantically asking for help when they've had a sudden change after a cold, or they developed tinnitus and had no answers. I am forever grateful that I can offer support to anyone who needs it. I have a hidden handicap, so often people don't understand what a day in my life is really like.

Each day is still a major struggle as my brain tries to hear. It strains my mind to listen, so I become exhausted faster than most people every day. Sometimes I feel like an outcast because if Jesse has friends over, sometimes I go up to bed earlier. It is hard to get used to those changes, as I used to dance and stay up late and listen to music. Now music makes hearing people harder, and the notes don't sound beautiful like they once did. Imagine if you could never enjoy music again.

Just recently, Jesse and I had friends over, and we played a game where you look at a screen, see a word and then use phrases to try and get your team to guess the word. I remember sitting in the corner and my team had their backs to me and I was unable to make out a single word they were saying. Without warning, tears just started to fill my eyes and I felt my legs carry me up the stairs, and I never went back downstairs. I couldn't do it. I went and lay next to my sleeping son and heard the beats of the music echoing up the stairwell, followed by roars of laughter. I lay crying next to my son thinking about how different my life was before all my challenges.

Staying stuck there is not who I am though, and most hours of most days, I find myself filled with a much deeper sense of joy than I have ever experienced before. I have a new lease on life, as the expression goes. My glass is always half full and I often think how grateful I am when conversing with anyone; simply because I can. Having lived three long months in total silence was so scary and so lonely that what I have seems like the best thing in the world. What is better is that I have learned to appreciate what most take for granted. Every day as I walk, I find myself feeling gratitude for that ability. When I look at my children, I feel increasingly thankful for the gift of vision. I feel this way because I used to think hearing loss was merely a byproduct of growing old. Never in a million years would I have thought there was even a tiny chance that I would be a deaf person.

Life is what you make it and how you choose to take your experiences and view them changes everything. If I were to view myself as a person with a handicap, then I would forever be that person. I make a choice each day about how I want my challenges to affect me. I make that choice when I get out of bed. Will I let it defeat me or will I have a sense of humour about it? The truth is, my brain has adapted so well that most people don't know I have a hearing problem at all. Sometimes I miss a word, and if my brain doesn't get it the first time, it can be repeated up to ten times, but until you spell it, it won't register. Not sure what happens there, but my brain shuts down and can't get it. Either way, I have to make light of it and make a joke to whoever I'm speaking with, and disclose that I have an implant. I have learned that owning it is far better than hiding it.

The people that I used to know well have split into two groups. Those who cared and those who didn't think I'd be useful to them as a deaf person, so they no longer came around.

That could be depressing if I really looked at it for what it is, but at the same time, I feel so blessed to have even tighter bonds with those that showed up, and I'm grateful for the amazing new friendships that I have developed being the new me.

Are there days when I crumple into a ball and cry because it's just hard? Yes, there are many such days. I wish more people took time to pull me aside and make more of an effort to make me feel included or comfortable when the environment is getting loud or I am sitting out alone. However, feeling sorry for myself does not help. Those sad events or realizations actually serve me, because the next day I wake up even more determined to make greater things happen in my life and to overcome bigger hurdles. It propels me to get up and be the best version of myself I can be.

The dark days have been able to create a very bright future. I still envision myself as a speaker, standing on a stage, helping empower those who find it hard to rise up from life's challenges. I want to be a voice for those who have a silent handicap. Pain is not visible to the naked eye, and pain is crippling. There are millions of people walking this earth who live with chronic pain conditions from autoimmune diseases. They need encouragement sometimes to carry on. I want to create community and a give them someone they can relate to and know they are not alone. If I can help even one person see a new way to view their challenge, to be able to stand up and get the help they need and deserve, then my hearing loss journey may have a greater purpose.

# CHAPTER EIGHTEEN

# Reflection

Reflecting on my many lonely and desperate days in the hospital, I can't help but feel gratitude for the doctors and nurses who saw that my suffering was real and treated me as a human. There were often times when I just needed an ear, as I missed my children and my husband, and some went way above and beyond to ensure I was comfortable and well cared for.

On the other hand, I need to address the reality, which was that other times I cry just thinking back to how poorly I was treated by a small handful of nurses. The way I was treated was deplorable. It was so inhumane that as I write this, I actually have tears in my eyes. Sometimes, I would enter the ER and I could see the nurses gathering to whisper about me. They passed judgment and thought I came in because I was addicted to the anti-nausea medication Gravol, or my lifesaving pain-relieving drug, Morphine. It was either that, or that I wanted attention. Despite always having serious symptoms that were visible, such as the time when I had Bell's palsy and half my face was drooping and I couldn't speak properly, they still talked about me and assumed I had some kind of mental issue. Sometimes I would open my mouth and show them the painful mouth ulcers, hoping that that they would somehow offer some empathy, but I was wrong. There were times in the process that I would unwillingly swallow my own saliva and scream in pain and they would think I was faking and would doubt my condition. Often it was the whispers that hurt the most, but sometimes it was the way I was spoken to.

One time, I came in via ambulance and I was vomiting non-stop while simultaneously having watery diarrhea. The nurse that was handed my case knew me well, and she was not pleased to be assigned to me when I arrived. I was so weak and sick that I couldn't even sit up. I had absolutely zero control over my bowels; as if I wanted to be lying in my own watery stool. I was shivering and cold, and as she walked in, she threw a bunch of towels on top of me, along with a diaper, and yelled at me. "Clean yourself up Monique! I'm not doing it!" I was literally lying in my own feces for several hours, still unable to control my bowels at all. It was like water was pouring out of me continuously. Every so often, she came in and scolded me to clean myself up again, while I lay helpless to act. I pleaded with her to help me, and each time she berated me and said there was no way she was going to clean me. That was one of my lowest points in my life.

That incident occurred before my diagnosis of Crohn's, and I guess with my underlying disease, catching a stomach bug was ten times worse for me. I ended up getting help from another nurse and a doctor I pleaded with who clearly saw my dire condition and came to my aid. It was one of the most degrading experiences ever. I was helpless, and all I could think about was how no one there respected me. I kept thinking about how in the outside world, I was perceived as a strong, successful woman that many people admired, but in there, I often felt pathetic and weak. It was such a strange and horrible experience.

Thankfully, I was often far too sick to care what they were saying, and finally getting diagnosed and cured hopefully made them feel awful for how they behaved. It got so bad at one point I had to send a letter to hospital management, who subsequently apologized and placed a note in my file stating that I must be treated with proper care.

Being yelled at when you are bleeding to death or being berated or told you are anxious when you are literally too weak to move your limbs is not okay. It will become another one of my life's missions to help advocate for the sick or weak people who are too helpless to advocate for themselves. Ironically, that particular nurse has since become very warm and kind to me. In fact, by the end of her shift, she already turned things around and must have felt remorse. I see her on occasion near the hospital, and she gives me warm smiles and we talk.

I remember another nurse who treated me bad so many times, and then one day she showed up at my bedside and just began to cry. She told me she was sorry, and I forgave her that instant, as I have forgiveness in my heart for the other nurse who didn't want to help clean me. I find forgiveness to be the best way forward and that harboring anger and resentment only hurts me. I have never been in a health care worker's shoes, so I cannot judge. I do feel, however, that it takes the right kind of person to care for sick patients. That person needs to be patient and exercise compassion for unwell people, and resist the personal need to pass judgment.

I have come so far since those days when the ER was my second home. When each night I'd go to bed not knowing if several hours later I'd be waking my husband and telling him I was going back in. For a while it became the norm, and he would get up in his sleep, walk me to my car, and go back to bed. Those days were lonely and filled with despair. I always hung my head in shame, walking in and praying I would end up with a nice nurse who believed I was sick. The only way to make it through life, when you feel there is no way out, is to learn to just trust. I believe we are all on our own life's path, and the general direction of the path is kind of set for us. If we can trust we are being guided down that path for a greater purpose, we can learn to withstand anything.

I kept up hope because I strongly believed that my suffering was purposeful, and if that is true, then perhaps it was so I could learn something that would ultimately enhance my life and allow me to fulfill my greatest wishes.

Can you imagine how beautiful it is to lose your hearing, and later actually feel blessed because of it? I can now appreciate my life in ways that, before my hearing loss, were not possible.

When your path takes an unexpected sharp turn, it is often very unsettling for us during that time, but oftentimes we look back and see how the experience inadvertently helped us. Like so many people, I took my day-to-day life, and more importantly my health, for granted. Only now, after overcoming so many shocking health crises, am I truly able to see the love that unconditionally surrounds me. That is the gift that I was given. It always existed, but I had not truly seen it.

The relationship I have with my husband is the most beautiful relationship I have ever encountered. He is the true definition of what I always imagined a best friend to be. He is always there for me, and his love and care has never wavered, even when his days became increasingly stressful because illness ran our lives. He has never doubted me or the extent of how bad I felt. He always put his needs aside to make me comfortable, and he never made me feel like I had better hurry up and get better or he'd hand me my walking papers.

When I used to see despair in his eyes when he came to my bedside, it was not because he was frustrated that he married a dud, it was because he hurt to see me hurt.

My deafness and Jesse had given me the greatest gift any human could ask for: love. I stated at the beginning of this story that you need to be careful what you wish for because some-times you have no idea how you will get to your end goal. You can visualize anything, and it can happen, but the path to get there is unknown, and it may not always be rosy on the way. I am so grateful to have this awareness, which has allowed me to flourish and navigate through my darkest days.

Attitude really is everything. If I was in a car accident and suddenly lost the use of my legs, would I sit and mourn my ability to walk? Absolutely! I would have very dark days and I would feel depressed at times, but I would also use my handicap to inspire as best I could.

I know one such person, who at age eighteen was hit by a car and has remained in a wheelchair for the past twelve years. While I have witnessed firsthand his personal battles with depressed feelings, he makes a choice each day to inspire. He is living on his own and has secured a beautiful, wheelchair friendly condo in the heart of the city. He enjoys the nightlife, plays wheelchair hockey, and exercises regularly. He has women that want to date him and don't see him as a man in a wheelchair. Rather, they see him as a man who has strength and a zest for life that is contagious. I can imagine his life, and I can feel many emotions that he would feel, even if our handicaps are not the same. We share a common denominator, and that is sudden loss of some-thing that most humans take for granted. We want it back, and we feel envy when we see those around us without the handicap. We also share a determination for not letting our challenges beat us.

In order for me to carry on and exist in my new life as a woman with on-going health issues, I have learned to live in the moment more. I never know what tomorrow will bring to my health. I am now a deaf woman and have Crohn's disease, and both afflictions will, with certainty, bring me unknown adversity. I know that, and I love and accept myself as I am. The nature of my issues will cause physical and emotional pain, but on a day when I feel none or I hear well, I celebrate. I liken my life now to seeing a show on a color TV vs black and white.

I'm not on autoplay anymore. No longer do I assume when I drive away for a day of work that I'll see my loved ones again. I could be killed in a car accident. I hug my children more, I express kind words to strangers more often, and I smile more. How many people reading this live like a factory worker? Do you wake up and stumble out of bed, listening to the tape in your head telling you how much your life sucks? Do you start your day by looking in the mirror and telling yourself that you look like crap, you've aged, and you need to lose a few pounds? Then do you look out the window and complain to yourself about the bad weather? You get dressed and kiss your spouse on the cheek like it's a chore on your way out the door. You go to a job you actually hate and think about how much you hate it and you complain about it often. You eat a fast overpriced, unhealthy meal, go home angry, and complain to your spouse because you hated sitting in traffic.

It's the same routine day in and day out. You put the punch card in and then punch out without noticing the destruction you're creating in your own life. You are your own worst enemy and if you don't take control of that, you will die without having the chance to really live. Your life is passing you by and you don't even notice the patterns you are creating.

Sickness sucks but it wakes us up. I tell everyone that will listen that they should know that nothing they have in their life now will necessarily be there tomorrow. A spouse can cheat and leave you without warning. Your kids are growing up so fast that the pirate face your son made for the past five months just stops happening. One day, you'll never have another Christmas dinner with your Mom. It all happens, so make a choice to start living the life that you are lucky enough to have.

Don't wait for a crisis to reignite the spark within you. We all deserve happiness and, more often than not, happiness is all around you, but you are unable to see it.

There are so many divorces these days — it's an epidemic. You obviously chose that person and vowed to stay with them until death do you part for a reason. The issue is that you likely married them because they brought you added joy and enhanced your life at that time. The relationship was new and so it helped to fill your seemingly empty cup. When the newness fades, kind of like you feel driving your new car three weeks post purchase, you become a factory worker in your marriage. Make out sessions become cheek kisses, and daily sex becomes monthly or quarterly sex. You resent most things they do, even though those same actions drew you to them in the first place. You crave newness because your life is becoming old, and that is because you fail to see the blessings that exist in the now.

Imagine if you looked at your spouse differently. Imagine if you saw them as loyal for being next to you on the journey called life. Imagine if you chose to make them feel good each day and treated them with love and care. Imagine if you awoke again and regained appreciation for your partner and began to focus on the positive things they do rather than the negative.

When you become ill, you are thrust into survival mode and somehow you can clearly see all the places you fail. Suddenly, you are grateful for that partner who is there by your side, who is equally bored but still hangs in there. The grass is not greener! The garden in front of you needs tending to, and it can create many beautiful blossoms. Affairs never work, and a new partner will inevitably let you down too, in time, when the newness wears off. No one can possibly make you see or feel lasting joy but you. To put your neediness onto a partner is unfair, and you can only put on an air for so long before your personal cracks begin to show.

I lie in bed every night now with my two-year-old son. Before, when I was sick, it was a chore of sorts. Yes, I enjoyed it, but I didn't cherish it because I felt too sick; and there is a big difference. Now I cherish the time I have with my son each night; putting him to bed is a gift. He is a blessing and he brings me so much joy. I never want to rush out anymore and finish a chore or go lie down. Now, the chore can wait. Now that I'm well, I can immerse myself and stay fully present with him. I know this precious time is fleeting. He will grow fast and won't snuggle his mommy anymore. I will never take this time for granted again.

Once I developed this new appreciation for my life, I also developed a stronger connection with myself. Instead of beating myself up if I have a bad day or berating my body for crapping out on me, I thank my body for pulling me through the illness and thank my brain for relearning to hear so well with the implant. The body is remarkable at healing and adapting to change. A dog with three legs can eventually walk and run like any other dog because it can adapt. The most important thing is to stay grateful and present and allow the dark days to occur. Humanize those dark days, and tell yourself that ups and downs are part of the human experience.

The words "this too shall pass" are truly words to live by. If you have an anxiety attack, the worst thing you can do is attach to the panic feeling because it exacerbates it. I find when I humanize the sensation by calling a spade a spade and acknowledging that I am having a panic attack, it will, like magic, just subside. Now, I never have them because I so often tell myself that "this too shall pass". They always do. We don't walk around in full panic mode all day. Worst case; it lasts an hour. Knowing that most really bad situations are followed by good ones allows healing on a deep emotional level.

When the relationship with your first true love ended, your heart was broken and it seemed like life was over. You thought you would never see a good day again. You lay in sweatpants on your sofa watching reruns and told yourself repeatedly how you must not be worthy. Food tasted bad, friends were not important, and almost everything you used to love was no longer joyful. The TV of life you used to see in color was all black and white. In time, you moved past it because you have the remarkable ability as a human to heal. You eventually find love again, and you look back with disbelief that you spent precious hours crying over that ex. Don't waste precious moments of your life. Allow despair. Humanize your situation and give it the energy and thought it deserves and then find your silver lining. The sooner the better. You don't have time to waste.

Before going deaf, I had closets full of acquaintances that I called friends. I socialized with people that did things behind my back that were hurtful because they were jealous of some aspect of my life. Maybe I earned more at the time, or a boy they wanted liked me instead. I had these women around me who I knew were doing hurtful things to me, and yet I would accept that behaviour because I was recently divorced, and I thought it was better to have some form of a social life than none at all. The truth is that you are in charge of your happiness, and if you allow others to treat you poorly, then you are reinforcing to yourself that you are not worth more.

Today, I would rather have one friend than ten frenemies. I cleaned house and I made a choice not to allow anyone in my space that impacts me negatively whatsoever. If they are not serving me by aiding me in my already-tough-enough journey, then they are out. I have no time to waste and that applies to my social scene now, too. I don't want to live in a façade at all in my life; ever. What you see is what you get. I now appreciate myself and feel that those who I call my friends are lucky. I used to feel lucky if someone wanted to spend time with me even if I knew they were two-faced.

Those who really like me for who I am made time for me and visited me when I was sick and learned that I was going deaf. Those who didn't care about me never showed up for me because as a deaf person, I was no longer going to be useful to them. Sadly, that's how you learn who your friends are, but I could have predicted in advance who would have come before it even happened. Don't wait to clean out the friendship closet.

Most of my life, aside from sleeping, was spent in the work-force. You would think that I would have chosen jobs that I like, but most of us don't, and I was no exception. I had countless jobs that I hated, and the thought of going to work was torture. Now, I make it my life's mission to get people to change careers they hate.

Recently, I had a friend come back from Australia, where he spent four years studying law and became a lawyer. When he came back to Vancouver, he began practicing law and withdrew completely. He never visited, was never at social gatherings, and when we saw him he seemed quiet and introverted. That was a far cry from the extrovert we all remembered. He confided in us that he had become a lawyer, but he hated every aspect of his job. The idea of the work and the long hours detracted from his existence. He lost a part of who he was.

Instead of allowing it to go too far, he made a personal choice to recognize where the unhappiness was coming from, and he chose to change his situation. He began by quitting law, and then he created a website and started selling items from his home on-line. He slowly found more joy as he saw himself taking back control of his life. He asked himself what he liked, and he created it. He has since become a mortgage broker and will begin a podcast to share insight about the ins and outs of the business. The change in him is astonishing. He smiles now, and he shows up to any social situation with a positive glow that is contagious.

Ask yourself every day, "If today were my last day on earth, what would I want to do differently?" and then do it!!!

Life after becoming deaf has been challenging to say the least. Until new technological advances present themselves, I will need to do what humans do so well; adapt. I have learned to show up more for my family and friends, and have thankfully gained a newfound appreciation and zest for life. By standing so close to death's door, I decided the time was now to live my entire life fully by honouring myself more and appreciating my remarkable existence.

I love the weather. Rain, snow, sleet, or hail. It is all beautiful. We will all die, and we will all feel pain and experience challenges, but I learned that there is always a silver lining. It is prudent that I live each moment and help others to see the detriment when they allow disparaging thoughts to drive them each day. If you are a doctor and you hate your job and would rather wait on tables, then I encourage you to do that. Find the good again in the loyal partner that you once vowed to grow old with. Rid yourself of those around you who are using you and whom you know would disappear if you no longer had anything of value.

Smile more and become less focused on what you don't have because if you are above the ground you have so much! Struggles are part of the human experience. Illness, death of a loved one, breakups, being let go from a job you loved, can happen and will happen, but sometimes when you exit the seemingly endless tunnel of darkness, you reawaken to a new and better version of yourself.

Your thoughts are your future, whether you believe it or not. The way you think will result in what you create. Be careful what you wish for. Find the blessings in everything bad and ask yourself what the lesson might be.

I used to be wild and careless. Yes, I could sell and make money, and on paper, I was a success. What is success though? I was flighty and was not grounded at all. I was going through the motions like a factory worker. I wasn't as present as I would have liked to have been in my first child's life because I was busy looking to make more money in my job and trying to find my true love. I made fake friends, whom I knew were fake, but I still chose to be around them because I felt that was all there was.

I don't look at those years as wasted though, because I can humanize what I was doing. To be forty-five and awake is huge! I see some of the fake friends I once had, and they remain in the same patterns, so it only serves to elevate my own personal sense of empowerment. I am my own best friend. I came into this world alone and I will die alone. I am responsible for my own happiness and can look nowhere and to no one but myself for fulfilment. I am still a major work in progress. I have days when I cry like a baby and I want to jump off the nearest bridge when I'm left out because I can't hear, or I miss events I used to love because it would be too hard to be there.

I struggle with insecurity, even though I have a great marriage. My mind chatter still exists; "Maybe he'll leave because I am a burden, or I don't produce deals the way I used to." As a human, I know that having unconditional love can exist, but it can be hard to believe even if it's right there. As a society, we are taught that a handicap is a handicap and those who have them are "different." I feel "different."

I don't care what people think of me anymore because ultimately, I only answer to me and not them. I have to face myself each day and be satisfied with how I chose to live that day. Did I live it feeling sorry for myself? Some days I do. I still take out my frustration about my challenges on my loved ones, but I ultimately humanize my experience and trust that knowing what it is that I'm doing is half the battle. I have several more tools in my life's toolbox thanks to my sudden deafness. I am grateful for my awareness and I hope that even one person can take inspiration from my challenges and live a more meaningful life.

# CHAPTER NINETEEN

# Trust

I have learned from experience that if I believe in something enough, I can manifest it into reality; especially if I back up my desires with feelings about my desire, and the vision of myself living with my desired outcome as if it has already occurred.

When Jesse and I made the decision to pursue IVF back in 2016, we made two perfect grade A embryos. Jack was selected by the doctor during my first IVF transfer in 2016, and we elected to freeze the other embryo so we could attempt to have it at a later date. We were clearly over the moon when I fell pregnant with Jack after one try and since my health was better, we felt confident that we wanted to add one more family member.

I had to go see all my doctors and specialists, and make sure they all gave me the green light and would watch over me and care for me should any issues arise. I made it through a series of hurdles and roadblocks, and felt certain that this embryo would take. I just knew our family was missing a member, and I knew I was going to have one more child in my care.

I was so confident that I have the fourth bedroom in my home set up as a nursery, and even have the baby clothes hung in the closet, awaiting the impending arrival. We were so lucky to get pregnant with one try in our IVF journey, that we failed to realize maybe how lucky we were, and how so many people never have a successful round after years of trying.

The day came to do the implantation and Jesse and I arrived at the clinic with bells on. Never have I met a man who loves little babies more than Jesse. It made having another one so exciting for us. We giggled away behind the curtain as we prepared for our turn to be implanted.

The moment came, and we watched on the screen as the doctor showed us our little embryo. It had survived the thaw, which was half the battle. We watched as she carefully placed the embryo inside my perfectly plumped up uterus (thanks to the assistance of hellish hormones I had to take).

After you leave, you feel worried that it's going to fall out or you'll pee it out, but you don't. You just don't. Once it's in, it's up to fate. The two-week wait is hellish. The first five days, you're happy and giddy with anticipation, but after day five, you feel a pull to pee on stick after stick, hoping to see the faint positive. I saw that faint positive on day five post-transfer with Jack.

This time I was not that lucky, and by day seven, I was a basket case of negativity, asking the clinic doctor to please give me a blood test to ease my mind. Well, it was negative too. I convinced myself I was having a baby, so I felt like it was impossible to not have a positive. Why was this happening? I was on a roller coaster of emotions because I felt so sure that I was going to mother another baby. I waited all the way to twelve days post transfer before I finally put myself out of my misery. I gave up hope and realized that it was not meant to be.

I surprised myself, though, with my strength and courage at that point. I'm not sure how or where it came from, but I felt a comfort this time. I felt like I was protected from a possible bad outcome or perhaps another slew of health issues. Who knows what was in that Pandora's box? What I know is that there is ALWAYS a silver lining, and mine was that we would now consider adoption. We decided that we would adopt a baby if this embryo didn't take. We knew when it failed that we were being directed onto another path. I am still determined to see my desires manifest, but just how I will get there is beyond my control. Just like many years ago, when I asked God to help me find a story. I placed the order and I got my story, but the how and why are all variables.

Will I get to be a mom again? Probably yes, if I were to place my bet in Vegas. I don't know how yet, or when it will happen, but I do know that I have the ability to attract it into my life. It will happen in the way that is best meant to happen for all parties involved. That is beautiful. The way I handled this surprises me a lot, but it is mainly because I learned to trust that from valleys come peaks, and from sadness comes joy, and if you trust that your path is purposeful, and learn to let go and release your need to control the how's and why's, then ultimately everything always falls into place.

# Final Notes

If I could go back to the life I had before going deaf, knowing what I know now, I would do so many things differently. I would certainly become a better listener. I would lie in stillness and enjoy silence, and I would cherish music even more than I did. Having said that, I have often asked myself if I would go back to my life before and the answer is actually—no. I like the new me better. I feel special, in a way, because of my challenges. I feel very lucky and blessed that I had such a catastrophic thing happen to me; it served as a massive wake up call. It felt like my life was truly over.

To be given another shot at hearing after living in sudden and total silence is like nothing any words I could type could accurately describe. I have a constant stream of gratitude flowing through me each day as I navigate my way through life. Every day, I have times when I have no clue what people are saying because they are not directing their conversation at me. I relax though, people watch, and know that when they want to reach me, they will look at and speak to me. I'm more relaxed because I have a new awareness about my life and how fleeting it can be.

The brain is so remarkable, and I am blown away by how quickly mine was able to adapt. Before the implant surgery, I was thrust without warning into a life of lip reading and the fact that I managed so well was astounding, really. I just adapted and was able to communicate almost normally when in a one-on-one situation. When I lost my balance and my world seemed to bounce up and down when I walked, my brain worked overtime so I could once again drive my car and walk without staggering.

When I finally received my implant and they switched me on, my brain was inundated with sounds coming from all angles. At first, "we" (my brain and I), had no idea what those sounds were. As an added challenge, I only had a single-sided implant, so we also had no idea where the sound was coming from. It was just sound or noise. An airplane overhead, my dog's bark, a lawn mower next door, or the doorbell, were all sounds that I had to relearn. I had to ask people, "What is that sound?" When they told me, I would think about how I remember hearing that sound and after enough repetition, I would eventually hear that sound exactly as I did before.

Today, I can't hear perfectly on the phone. I only catch about 80 percent. Certain voices, like my mother's or Jesse's, I can hear clearly because I hear them most often. I also don't feel flustered and nervous talking to them because I know I can ask them to repeat themselves and they won't be judgmental. I am constantly seeing improvements in the way I perceive sound, and for that I am grateful. I have the hope that one day there will be improved technology which might allow for me to hear even better and perhaps even enjoy the sound of music once again.

In my day-to-day life, I still perceive limitations as I can't hear as well as I once could. I withdraw at times from social situations, especially when those I am with seem to care less whether I hear them well or not. There is a distinct difference to me with the way certain people treat me now when compared to how they treated me before. Some friends take the time to sit with me face to face and make sure I feel included, while others just worry about themselves.

Interestingly though, I've had a few calls over the years from very affluent people who are socially very strong who had suffered a sudden decline in one of their ears. Single sided deafness is actually very common and can happen without warning. They heard about my hearing loss and reached out for help. When I met one woman in particular, she had barely spoken to me when we worked together in the past, but one day she invited me for lunch. Amid her despair, her walls came down, and she opened her heart to me and expressed fear about her hearing loss on the one side. I calmed her down and explained that she still has one natural hearing ear, and with that she could be 100 percent okay and still enjoy all life has to offer. With the natural hearing she still had, she would still hear birds, music, and the phone clearly. She was far from dire in my eyes, but she didn't see it that way because hearing with two ears was all she knew. She will likely never lose the other ear, and will eventually totally adapt to single-sided deafness. In the wake of that personal devastation, she retired from work and decided to travel the world. She has a new-found appreciation for her life and a softness about her now which was never there before.

Adversity and change are not easy, but it is how we learn to perceive it that is important when moving forward. The understanding that there are many people in the world that have it a thousand times worse than me helped me move forward with acceptance and even gratitude. I would think of how much worse it could be. Was I dying of cancer? Was I in a wheelchair? The caring people who took the time to reach out to me will have places etched forever in my heart. Those who turned their backs on me or heard about my deafness and never even sent me a text did me a favour because they prevented me from wasting another moment of my precious life with them.

I am free now; no longer a prisoner of my life bound by the demands of the factory worker mentality. I find beauty and pleasure everywhere and every day from the simplest things. I still overcome personal hurdles often and have moments where I feel sorry for myself. Being human is hard, and the sooner we accept that, the better. I hope my journey continues to be anything but mundane. I'm invigorated and excited to see tomorrow and what it will bring. I challenge you to awaken your senses and learn to appreciate them again before, without warning, one is taken away. Know that if something catastrophic were to happen — you can make it through.

I never thought this would happen to me, nor did I ever think that eventually I would be this happy because of it. There is always a reason why something happens, and we can almost never see why at the time. Trust that there are no accidents, and that your life has a purpose. One day, the answer will reveal itself in the most beautiful way, and you will awaken to see the gift and resulting beauty in your life.

Before I end my story, I want to share with you the lessons I've learned.

# The Lessons I've Learned

## Manage Stress

One of the worst parts about suffering an unexpected illness or traumatic event is the untimely nature of when it appears in your life. A simple sprain of your ankle can turn your world upside down. You don't realize how much you use that ankle until you try to put pants on while balancing on one leg, carrying a child, or using the gas and brake pedals in the car.

By our very nature, we are programmed to live a fast-paced life, wherein the idea of slowing down and not completing our daily list of tasks is not an option, so the concept of stopping to allow ourselves to heal is unfathomable.

When you are not given a choice, it creates mental turmoil as you try to find your footing. Your mind chatter tries to take over and, rather than help you, it tries to bring you down. That creates added stress in addition to the normal ongoing stress you already deal with for your day to day survival. I didn't realize how much stress I was under until I was forced to stop literally everything and take inventory.

What I discovered was eye-opening. It changed my entire perception of my life. You see, I am a perfectionist, and because of that trait, I found myself to be particularly vulnerable to stress. I was always just on the brink of being completely overloaded. How many people do you know that, when they reach that point, seem to come down with the flu or have an accident or something else when it is the worst possible time. Or is it?

Is that nature's way of slowing us down when we simply have too many irons in the fire? I believe that I created that stress myself by falsely believing that somehow, without me doing something perfectly, the world would somehow suffer. That is of course false, and I quickly learned that if I took myself out of the equation, the sun would still rise and set without my help.

I began to understand that I am not separate from the whole and since things are moving all around me with or without my help, I can relax and just allow; almost like floating on your back in a moving stream and just allowing your body to ebb and flow with the currents.

The release of control was needed for me, as I really and truly had none. Ironically, the idea that I was part of a whole came to me while I was in total isolation. I could no longer struggle or even make an effort to exist in my old life, but somehow things took care of themselves without my help. It was interesting to observe. It became important for my recovery that I stop being a doer, and relax, and allow. In doing everything all the time, I was inadvertently creating a life filled with tension, stress, and anxiety about meeting deadlines.

I saw that stressful world as my only reality and was unable to relax without the stress. It's like watching my teen daughter try to exist for even 30 minutes without touching her smartphone. In her world, that's not possible.

The way the Universe operates is very simple: if you are burning your candle at both ends, it will simply step in and intervene without warning.

## Expect the Unexpected

If you knew you would never see your loved one again, would you change the way you said goodbye? You always hear people say that since you never know when you'll see someone again, leave them peacefully and tell them you love them, so should the unexpected occur, you can feel good about how you left them.

Whenever a tragedy occurs, it truly changes the lens through which you see the world. I know with every health challenge I've faced, I always took something away from it which made me feel like I had grown deeper and wiser as a human being. My lens would change and where I placed emphasis on what used to be important began to shift. I saw my loved ones as such gifts, and I changed the way I treated them. I loved them all so much before, but when you're near death, you really see clearly just how much you love them, and how having the last word is not important. I must admit, sometimes I still fall victim to my negative mind chatter, and I can take my feelings of sadness out on my loved ones. I certainly don't want to, and I have awareness now about how I need to live and spend my hours only with those who truly are caring souls that genuinely like me. I also know that time goes by fast, people grow, and what I have today may change tomorrow without warning.

As I write this today, I just returned home from two weeks in and out of the hospital. It began a month ago when I noticed that the diastolic blood pressure number, which is the bottom number, was slowly creeping up. I have a monitor because when I nearly bled to death the first time, the long wait for blood caused infarctions (areas of dead tissue) to occur on each kidney. As a result, my perfect kidneys lost function and since kidneys affect blood pressure, I keep a watchful eye.

I mentioned this to my specialists, but they shrugged it off and said I was fine. One day I felt off while playing with Jack. I did a quick check and was alarmed when I saw 180/120 staring back at me. My normal was 115/75.

I immediately packed up the baby and headed for the nearest clinic, where there, too, I was met with a gross lack of concern. She told me maybe I have anxiety and that it might be just that. I was shocked. I insisted there was something wrong and she then told me that perhaps I just had high blood pressure and would need to start blood pressure medication. I did not find it reasonable that I would develop hypertension overnight without some serious urgent medical issue being the cause.

I drove over to the ER and had my mother-in-law meet me there to take Jack home. Here we go again, I thought. Of course, at this point my philosophy of just going with the flow were tossed out the window as my fight-or-flight response kicked in. I knew I had one chance to state my case to the ER doctor, and I knew that having the right doctor would make all the difference.

I faced the usual stares from some of the nurses, while others gave me a gentle smile. Seven hours later, after I was given some blood work and an ECG, I was told something I already knew. I was not having a heart attack. I told the doctor about my kidney issues, but he told me my blood work showed no decline in my renal function and, despite me asking for an ultrasound to look at my kidneys, or bloodwork to test my adrenal function, he denied me and told me to go see my internist in a few days.

I knew that whatever was happening was either a growth or tumour in my pituitary gland or adrenal glands, or an issue with my kidney, as all the above mentioned directly affect blood pressure. I had also recently put on ten pounds (that distinctly felt like fluid), felt pain and pressure behind my eyes, (my vision had changed slightly, requiring glasses), and I had a lot of headaches and some random joint pain. I'd chalked it up to possible side effects from my Crohn's' medication. Now, I was certain that something was really wrong.

A few days later I saw my internist, and he ordered more blood tests. I asked him to check my adrenal and pituitary glands to rule out hormonal causes. All the tests came back within three days, except one test for aldosterone and renin. These hormones are secreted when the kidneys or adrenals are under stress and the ratio is usually off when a tumor is present on the adrenals. In a way, I was hoping for an abnormal result so it could explain away all my issues. I called the lab and was told that the test took up to fifteen days to return.

In the meantime, I tried to go on with my life; despite feeling short of breath easily and having weakness in my legs climbing stairs. One night, I woke up gasping for air, and I'd had enough. This time, I drove to St. Paul's Hospital. I didn't want to have to face judgment and be dusted off again. I went in with guns blazing, and this time the doctor made me cry as she listed all the tests she would do to make sure I was safe. I finally felt heard and like I could relax.

As I lay on the stretcher in the hallway of this busy downtown hospital, my mind wandered. I saw so many patients come in; some on drugs, some homeless, and even prostitutes wearing evidence of a date gone bad. A man actually walked by my stretcher, smiled at me, took my Nike runners off the end, and started to walk off with them. The security guard stepped in and gave them back and then told me to watch my stuff, saying, "They will sell anything." It was shocking.

My mind took over and replayed the old tapes of me being sick and the what-ifs soon followed. I didn't want to go back to the constant sickness and the constant time away from my family. I knew that my family wouldn't manage easily with my absence. I thought for sure this was a thing of the past. My Crohn's was in full remission and my blood work had been amazing. The guilt then followed, as I lay there helpless to whatever my fate was. I wasn't thinking about myself; I was only worrying about how the issues might affect my family, and the burden it could place on them.

The doctor returned and told me my heart failure markers were elevated. What?! I was in total shock. She also told me that this may be only a false marker because the other tests and markers were normal. She suggested that it was because my heart was working very hard and producing a lot of this enzyme and that my kidney function, lower than average, was not clearing it fast enough. That may be true, but even if there was a chance I was in heart failure, that was the scariest thing to hear. She then wanted to send me home. She said that they had exhausted all the tests and that I should follow up with my internist.

I point blank refused. I refused to be sent home with my blood pressure staggeringly high. Was she for real? I demanded that she do more to find the cause. She was getting annoyed at this point and implied that I was worrying for nothing and just anxious and offered me an Ativan. I asked her if she would be anxious, too, if her heart rate had climbed to heart attack levels seemingly overnight, followed by an elevated heart failure enzyme test. She concurred and agreed to send in an on-call internal medicine resident and told me it would be their decision if they wanted me to go home. I would have no choice.

I agreed. Hours later, and flying high on Ativan, I was tapped on the chest by a small Asian woman. I could tell immediately that she had been coached and prepped by the ER doctor. She was likely told that I was fine, just anxious, and that I just had high blood pressure, which I should go home and deal with as an outpatient.

I summed up my case as best as I could. I was grateful for my many years in sales and my extensive medical Googling background, because I was able to convince her that a CT scan of my abdomen with contrast dye was needed. I hated that I had to fight to get this test. I also hated that I had to receive my 18th CT scan in five years. I just knew intuitively that they would find something wrong with my kidneys.

I was wheeled over to the trauma unit, which was far less interesting than the stretcher in the entry, but I felt one step closer to victory. Soon, Jesse, Jack, and Rachael arrived by my side, and almost simultaneously, the doctor called Jesse on his cell. The worst part was my attending nurse had approached us twenty minutes earlier saying the doctor wanted to talk to us about the tests and wanted to make sure we were all together.

When Jesse's cell rang, I think I practically hit Jesse in the face when I leapt up into a seated position. I saw a serious look on his face as he listened. I kept hitting him over and over, and asking him what she was saying. He looked at me and said the artery to my left kidney was blocked and that my left kidney was only 6.5 cm and should be eleven.

My heart sank in my chest. I tried to understand how this could have happened. My blood work showed no lessening of renal function. I had had side pain for a month or so, but thought it may have been a muscle spasm. I assumed this was a medical emergency, and that I would be prepped for surgery to try and save the kidney and open the artery.

When he hung up and I asked him what they planned to do. He said 'nothing'. He told me that the procedure to open the artery was too risky, and that the kidney had suffered too much damage to recover. It was as if the wind was completely knocked out of me. I was speechless, and if you ask Jesse, that truly never happens. I lay and sobbed and wondered why. When he then told me that this likely wasn't the cause of my high blood pressure, I snapped. Not at him, but at the very idea that something else was responsible. I was outraged. I knew with 100 percent certainty that this would prove to be the cause. The doctor admitted me to the hospital and told me they would look to find the cause of the hypertension with other tests, and they would ensure my blood pressure was controlled with medication before my release.

My biggest concern was that they would send me home on blood pressure pills, when three weeks earlier I had had perfect blood pressure, and say, "Have a nice life. More meds for you, Monique." I was not okay with that, and I was determined to make sure someone heard me.

I was poked and prodded for six long days and nights. I felt healthy this time, compared to when I had undiagnosed Crohn's and battled the C. difficile toxin for two years. It was worse this time, to be there feeling relatively good, because I wanted to get up and go. High blood pressure is dangerous though, so it forced me to stay put.

The doctors wanted me to start high blood pressure medication immediately, which was the last thing I wanted... another medication, but until they could find the cause, I felt I had no choice. With one functioning kidney, I didn't want the pressure to damage the other one, so I was brave and tried what they gave me. All the literature said that high blood pressure due to a renal artery dissection or tear is not easily controlled with normal meds. I kept voicing this, but it fell on deaf ears.

Every day, I went online and looked for the result of the aldosterone and renin test, and finally it arrived. I found it unusually hard to interpret. There was no red flag showing out of range, but there was also no range written next to the aldosterone. The comment below said that the ratio was normal and was not indicative of an adrenal tumour. I still wanted to know what a normal aldosterone number was. I had to Google it and convert pmol to whatever conversion I found. It showed me that it should be 200 or less. Mine was 965. I told the resident internist and she said she doesn't look at that number. She only looks at the ratio, and if the ratio is okay, then I have no tumour, so that's it.

I still felt that she was wrong, so I emailed my regular internist and asked him if this number was high. Too much aldosterone can be produced if your kidney is injured or damaged. It is the body's way of crying for help. The increased amount can cause you to retain sodium and fluid, which raises blood pressure. It can cause you to pee out too much potassium and mine was a bit low. It made sense to me that this was having an impact because I distinctly noticed the fluid retention and weight gain. It can also cause headaches, leg weakness, muscle pain, and even vision changes. I knew I had my answer, but how to convince the doctors?

Before I left, my kidney doctor came to see me. We discussed my options and I expressed my concerns. I told her that I felt my kidney issues were causing my high blood pressure and that conventional medication wouldn't help. I said that they should remove the kidney to ensure the signal stops, and my blood pressure could return to normal.

I told her that I wanted it dealt with urgently because I did not want to risk injuring the remaining lower functioning kidney. She agreed with me, but she reminded me that the surgery would need a meeting outside of the hospital with a urologist, and that we would need to convince him. She promised to follow me closely, monitor my pressure, and try to stabilize it with meds. I had no choice but to agree because removing a kidney was a big deal, even if it was not functioning well. Even dead kidneys are normally not removed, rather, transplanted ones are put in below them.

I went back home with lower but not well controlled pressure, and my pulse was crazy high. The average for me was usually 75 and now it was 100–125. I still felt really short of breath and just had a niggling feeling that something still wasn't finished.

I woke up in the morning and felt weak coming back upstairs after I went to get Jack a bottle. I told Jesse that I just had to go back to the hospital and be seen. I drove back across town because it was a shorter wait. I couldn't face the judgement I always faced at the local hospital, and they had a record of my recent history. They brought me in fast after I told the triage nurse that I had just spent a week there. They began with blood tests and an ECG again to check my heart. An hour later, I heard a nurse say, "Monique's potassium is 2.4." It was dangerously low, even life threatening; it should be 3.5-5.5. If you have very low potassium, it can cause a sudden heart attack. I was so lucky that I had the intuition that something wasn't right.

I was sent into the trauma unit and an internal medicine doctor was assigned to me. I was immediately given an IV and oral potassium. I could feel the improvements within a few hours except, of course, for the fast pulse and high blood pressure. Once again, the resident suggested there was nothing further to do and that I was safe to leave. I told him I wanted to stay until my potassium was stable and my blood pressure was in the safe zone. With reluctance, he admitted me.

My emotions were a combination of stealth determination, sadness, desperation, dread, fear, and guilt. The guilt was the most prominent. I didn't want my husband to feel like he would have more stress caused by me. After I was sent up to floor seven again, I reunited with many nurses who were surprised to see me back. I settled in behind my curtained off one quarter of a four-person room.

I kept researching. Two days later, my internist messaged me back from the email I had sent the week prior about my aldosterone. His reply was simple. He said, "Yes, Monique, that is high, and it may explain a few things." I told him that nothing was working, as far as the blood pressure meds that they had me on, and he said that I need to be on a potassium sparing beta blocker, on a low dose, and a drug called Spironolactone that blocks the aldosterone.

I instructed my doctors accordingly, and within two days, my pressure was far better, my pulse lower, and my potassium stable. I went home, and a week later, I was down a full seven pounds from no longer retaining so much fluid. Miraculously, I also no longer need glasses. It remains to be seen whether the kidney will need to be removed or if we will tweak the meds enough to keep my blood pressure normal until the kidney stops sending the alarm signals.

I was enjoying amazing health, and Jesse and I had just made more embryos, which I had been cleared by all the doctors to carry. Now without warning, after cashing in our retirement savings to pay for the genetically tested embryos, I can no longer safely carry a baby myself because of my advanced maternal age and only having one lower functioning kidney. As unexpected as this was, it happened. Because of what I have learned, I was able to shake this hiccup very fast.

I focused on the positive. I am still very healthy, and I was scanned head to toe and have no growths, cancers, or diseases that caused this. This was another unfortunate circumstance. While trying to find my Crohn's, my kidneys had been poked and biopsied so many times that we may have weakened that main artery. It's hard to know. I can't dwell on what happened because that would take time away from enjoying my life. I still feel vibrant, and my Crohn's is still in remission. Finding this high aldosterone was a win because my unexplained fluid retention, vision changes, muscle aches, and headaches are now gone.

Maybe I was being protected because me carrying the baby myself might have been too much for me. We will forge ahead. Now we will look into surrogacy, as we have our heart set on making a baby sibling to grow up with Jack.

## Be Your Own Advocate

It is so unfortunate that the medical system has failed me, personally, so many times. I am thankful that I have an able mind and the capacity to do my own research. What about those who cannot and are left helpless or sent home because the ER doctors are stressed out with too many patients and miss something hugely important? I often wonder if the first ER doctor had just granted me the kidney ultrasound I requested, and noticed some shrinkage in the kidney, if we could have saved some function.

It is so important to establish a baseline feeling in your body so if something is amiss you can take action. I suggest getting bloodwork tested as often as your health insurance will allow. Then educate yourself about what each marker means, and what a shift in one could mean. Keep records. It's your health, and it up to you to manage it. I know if my family gets sick and has a symptom, I can pretty much pinpoint exactly what it is and what tests could be taken to confirm the diagnosis.

Health is something that we all take for granted. I'm here to say that one day, when you least expect it, anything can go sideways. Always check your urine. Is it a normal colour, foamy, or smelly? I understand that this may sound strange, but simple changes, if caught early, can prevent a long list of major health problems down the line. Headaches, weight gain, mood changes and muscle aches that don't line up with activity or unexplained fatigue can all be signs of illness. Don't ignore the signs, and if you're a middle-aged woman and you suddenly gain ten pounds in a short span, don't let the doctors chalk it up to simple menopause! Ask for tests and make yourself be heard. The very notion that when I went to the medical clinic and two hospitals presenting with a 180/120 blood pressure and was told it was fine, likely just anxiety, is infuriating. Being sent home twice before they found a main renal artery collapse is also totally unacceptable.

I thought this was over and it wasn't. It was unexpected. I took something new away from this. I saw how my mind put me in to a total state of fear, which although understandable, did not serve me at all. I know that I need to release and surrender from now on when it comes to my health. I believe in a higher power. I know that I have a chosen path, and whatever comes along on my path, I have free will to choose how I handle it. The sooner I stop fighting against the tide, the better. As hard and alienating as it is to be sick, I can make peace with myself. I got to know myself; I came in alone and I will die alone. It sounds bleak, but it's the cold hard truth. I'm my own very best friend. I irritate myself, but I also take care of myself. I am a work in progress. I feel way more peaceful now than I did before the kidney injury. I feel far more protected and even more determined to find a way to get Jack's sibling into this world. I won't make myself crazy, though. I will release and surrender, and trust that whatever is meant to be will simply be.

I can only hope that my story serves as a wake-up call and provokes more self-awareness when it comes to your health. Without health, you really have nothing else.

## Stay Present

When I was going through each trauma, I always found myself trapped in a cloud of fear. The feeling of fear was a result of my mind racing all over the place and bombarding me with images of past traumas and bleak potential futures. How can you possibly stay present in the moment when your present moment is so scary?

I learned to *feel* and *observe* the fear, but not attach to it. The result was that I found myself able to be present. When you are aware of the processes that are currently taking place in your mind and body, then you are present as the observer; as long as you don't let the thoughts take over and send you into another place.

The best tool I learned to help me retrain my mind to focus on the here and now was to look at my surroundings, focus on an object around me and describe it to myself. An example would be if I was driving down the highway and found my mind wandering, I could look at the wheat colored grasses and describe their beauty. "The grasses are long, and they are wheat colored, and they are swaying in the breeze." When in a hospital bed, I looked at the pale blue curtain surrounding my bed and I think, "The curtain is thin and pale blue, and is not wrinkled." This technique of making observations about your current surroundings to keep you focused in the here and now. Staying present alleviates anxiety and somehow helps bring about a magical feeling of calm.

Although it sounds simple, this technique is actually a fairly difficult thing to master as day-to-day life requires planning, situations come up without warning, and it's hard to stop and point out colorful objects to yourself in the middle of it all. An easy way to reconnect is to use the time you spend in your car or at the gym as your spiritual workplace. I allow time each day to do this work, as it is mandatory for my mental and spiritual health. When I'm driving, instead of my mind using that time to torment me and bombard me with negativity, I exercise mind control. I begin by thinking about what makes me smile. My children, my husband, my mother. I say to myself, "Thank you for my family. Thank you for my beautiful home. I am grateful that I can hear and communicate…."

I concentrate on what I currently have, not what I want in the future. This exercise works beautifully, and it brings a smile to my face. The shift in my energy is instant, and is far better than if I'd spend my drive listening to negative chatter.

There is definitely a time and a place to visualize your future though, and I like to spend some of my day "manifesting my dreams." I like this exercise because I believe it works. It really feels good, like I have done something very meaningful for my life when I take the time to visualize the things I want to achieve.

While I'm imagining myself healthy and running around in my lakeside vacation home with my family, I focus on the feelings tingling through my body as if I am already there. I can feel the sun beating down on me, and I can hear the laughter of the children being chased around the yard by their dad. When I concentrate on those feelings, that's when I know my order has been placed and the wish is on its way. Doing my manifestations are a daily routine that forces my mind to stay present and positive as opposed to wandering to darker places.

I believe that this helps my life in so many ways. I feel positive because I feel a connection to a greater power. I feel like the very act of dreaming about beautiful, happy things allows me to tap into a small part of the feelings that are associated with that dream. Those feelings lift my energy up, and since like attracts like, I feel as though I set myself up for success.

If you have ever had a really bad day, it often starts with something small that doesn't make you happy. Maybe when you wake up, you have a headache and your mind starts to lament, "This sucks. I have a bad headache." Your mood shifts because you feel bad. You walk around getting ready for your day when you stub your toe. You swear. You snap at your child because they are not listening well to instructions. When you finally get to the car, the traffic is bad, and all the drivers seem to be pissing you off. The day just continues on a downward spiral because you don't realize that your mind is telling you how much everything sucks and it's dragging you further into the abyss. You are then attracting one bad thing after the other until you can regain control and get back into the present.

I am not a true master of always staying in the moment, but I do know the importance of it, and I've felt glimpses of the magic associated with its mastery. Having the awareness about the importance of not getting stuck in dark places of the mind is half the battle. We are all able to create our reality, but it takes discipline to devise effective routines to help us along the way. If at first you don't succeed, then try again and know that practice will eventually make perfect.

## Be your own "Ride or Die."

I have spent countless days, starting from early childhood, when I felt truly alone in this world, but it wasn't until forty-four years into my life that I learned that being alone does not have to be a negative. Most people spend the majority of their lives running away from themselves because they don't truly like themselves. When the mind has been left to run rampant for too long unchecked, the result can manifest in the form of panic attacks or depressed feelings, which creates a fear-based relationship with the self.

This can happen in so many ways. If you have a traumatic experience, you inevitably want to suppress it and tuck it away. You may bury it in your subconscious mind so you can put on a brave front and face the world. The issue is when you find that you cannot be alone because you are afraid you may have to deal with the thoughts that surface. That fearful feeling about being alone is harmful and can lead to substance abuse or other self-destructive patterns.

Self-love is something that has truly taken me forty-four years to practice. I used to look in the mirror every day and pick myself apart. "My nose is too big. I have a double chin. My calves are fat..." and I could go on.

Would you say that to your best friend? Why on earth was I saying that to myself when I already have a world full of haters all around me? My body underwent so many changes; when I had my most recent hospitalization, I had an epiphany. I thought, 'Wow, good for you, body! You fought so hard for me. You fixed my weird bouncy vision, and relearned to walk.' My brain even learned how to hear with this implant. I started to cry. I thanked my body from head to toe. I literally hugged this body. It is the home for my soul and without it, I would not be afforded this earthly experience. It truly is a temple and it deserves the praise that a temple receives. I often visualize the colour pink as loving energy coming from my heart, and I send that loving energy to all my organs and I thank them. I marvel at their strength and tenacity, especially, most recently, my kidneys.

I look in the mirror and I admire my beauty. It is unique, and it belongs to me. My big nose is perfectly imperfect, and it makes me who I am. My beauty comes from within me, and it radiates outward. Every day, I face judgement. Some people love me to the ends of the earth. They know I am a real person with real challenges and that I genuinely want to help other people. Others are suspicious of me. "Why is she posting her stuff on Facebook? Why does she think she's so great?"

With a world full of judgment, I knew I needed to get off the judgement bus and leave the haters to hate. I needed my own bus. My bus is filled with approval and compassion for myself. I understand myself and only I truly know what I mean when I say something, or what my true intentions are. I am no longer afraid to face myself. One by one, I can allow a fear to surface and change the way I perceive things. I can trust myself to make smart choices and I appreciate how far I have come. I can recognize my imperfections and my annoying tendencies now, but instead of criticizing them, I find them cute.

I had a history of very serious panic attacks that started when I was twenty-one. When they occurred, I felt as though I couldn't breathe, and my heart would beat so fast I thought I was having a heart attack. Looking back, the cause was me ignoring myself and not listening to my own intuition. I would numb pain by ignoring it or covering it with a quick fix, like a new haircut, or a new outfit.

Once I realized that hiding from what I know and not wanting to face it was the very cause of my panic, I began to face things and watched as the anxiety disappeared.

All my experiences have led me here. I no longer care who likes me or who doesn't. I don't care if my chin is a bit double. It doesn't matter. What matters is that when I am alone, I am in peace. I like hanging out with me. Who would have thought? Knowing I have my own back and trusting my inner guidance system, that I can clearly hear and feel, gives me great confidence going forward, that I can face any challenge that comes my way!

When life pushes me over, I'll push back harder. Life is a mystery that I'm no longer afraid to explore.

# No regrets!

Lying on a stretcher while trays of blood poured out of my GI tract left me scarred for life. Not just because my kidneys are literally scarred, but because the memory of actually believing I was going to die in that moment is etched forever in my mind.

While I lay there, helpless to the circumstances, I was able to reflect on my life and all the many things I regretted.

## 1. Turn off the technology

I wished I had turned off my smartphone more. Yes, as I lay dying, I lamented about the fact that my smartphone was too involved in my life and the lives of my teen daughter and spouse. It made me sad. I felt it was a modern-age devil that needed to be reined in.

## 2. Be happy with what you have

I wished I had spent more time enjoying what I have now, and not always looking for something more. So many people get stuck here. You think happiness will come from some material item or future event.

## 3. Listen to your intuition

I wished I had listened more to my inner guidance system. Knowing what I know now, I am certain that it always steers me in the right direction. Don't ignore a feeling, whether it's good or bad.

### 4. Leave no enemies

I wished I had made peace with people from my past that I had mistreated or unfairly passed judgement on.

### 5. Show more empathy

I wished I had exercised more empathy for people that have suffered hardships or who found themselves alone and in need of help.

### 6. Self-worth

I regretted that I gave too much of myself and bent over backwards sometimes for loser guys because I somehow built them up to be these gods that I would be so lucky to have a chance with.

### 7. Eliminate toxic people

I wished I had eliminated people from my life sooner that were toxic, negative influences. Knowing how fleeting life could be, I was almost angry that I allowed a day, let alone many days, of mistreatment in my life. There have been so many two-faced or fair-weather friends that have crossed my path in my life, and despite my better judgement, I would still spend time with them. That will not happen anymore.

# In Closing

These are just a few of the things that I wished I had done differently, and it was interesting to make a catalogue of them after I was fortunate enough to leave the hospital. I felt happy that in regard to my career, I had absolutely no bones to pick with myself.

I loved each job I have had throughout my life and was smart enough to sense when it was time to change direction. I cannot stress enough to anyone who is working, that each day spent in a job that brings you little to no joy is detrimental to your health. You can and should have passion for your work, and if you feel like you are dragging your heels every day to get there, then it's time to move on.

Don't wait for a tragic event to happen. Open your eyes and see that life is too short to not be living free from stress and in your happy place. I remembered thinking how many times I'd heard of bad things happening to people; how awful it was, but I never thought for a second it could happen to me. You never believe anything bad will happen to you, but knowing that even the smallest crisis can knock your life upside-down should give you pause to make sure you are exactly where you want to be.

## Celebrate the Sunsets

With every ending there is always a new, fresh beginning. Every time I closed a chapter in my life, even if it was hard, the sun always rose again. With it came new perspective. Sometimes endings come easily and are welcome, like a graduation or moving to a new home, but other times, endings are sudden and unexpected, like death or loss.

When I lay for three months in my bed, it was a huge ending for me. I never thought in a million years I would ever be happy or enjoy my life in any capacity, ever again. The sun kept rising and setting each day, and with each passing day, a new brighter perspective emerged. It always does. I could never see at the time why the bad things happened, but it's amazing how later on, I am able to look back and marvel at the positive impact the seeming devastation had on my life.

When I implanted my second and only remaining embryo, I assumed it would work in one try, like Jack. When it failed, I was beside myself. I had taken three months of hormones, and endured horrible hot flashes and mood swings. I refused to accept that this baby wasn't coming. At that time, I was angry at the world. I felt sad and shocked, and I also felt like, somehow, it wasn't fair. Friends would send me cryptic intuitive messages like "trust and allow" or "release and surrender" and I knew I had to, but I couldn't. I could not see anything positive at that time because we had set up the nursery and spent months looking for our dream home with 4 bedrooms to complete our family.

I had also been cleared by all my doctors to go ahead and try because they committed to closely monitoring me and ensuring my best care. I was so encouraged that my health was finally good enough and then it didn't work!

Jesse and I are convinced our little family is still missing one member, and unlike Rachael, who grew up alone, we wanted Jack to have a sibling who was close in age. We immediately set about looking into our options. We had just bought a big house and had no more funds to pay and make more embryos. It was not a simple process either.

We contacted several adoption agencies and there were two that were full and not accepting new prospective parents, and the one that was, was not so encouraging. They told us that most moms would likely want to give up their baby to a family that had no children, so their child would be the focus, and also to help make the parents' dreams come true. I understood that, but due to my age and Jack almost turning three, we decided against the possible wait of several years.

One day, it occurred to me that I could sell my RRSP and we could give it another try and make more embryos. We went down the path with the plan that I would go through the treatments again and carry the baby. We had just finished sending off the last payments to create our embryos when my kidney failed.

Can you imagine if that embryo in January had taken, and I would have been four months pregnant when my blood pressure hit 180/110? I would have lost the baby or my life! Could I have ever in a million years thought that not having the embryo implant was a blessing?

We now had a new issue, and that is that with one kidney and all these embryos, it's not safe for me at forty-four to carry. It could put my, and the baby's life, in danger. We also don't have $60,000 in extra cash to help pay an altruistic surrogate her expenses. So now what?

Just while I was knee deep in thought, I received a text that my friend's daughter has offered, out the goodness of her heart, to carry this baby for us. I was on the floor in a pool of tears, instantly. I could not believe that anyone could possibly be that selfless. My heart was so full. I was afraid it wouldn't work because the clinics require that the carrier has had at least one child of their own first to be a consideration.

For some reason, when I found out that she did not meet the requirements, I was still at peace. I know the universe has a plan for us, whatever that may be. I don't know today how my baby will come, but I know it will. Had this kidney thing not happened when it did, we would have suffered not only the loss of the kidney, but also the baby, and maybe even my life. Had the kidney thing happened even a day earlier, we would have halted the embryo creation, as we never would have made the embryos with the thought of also needing to find funds for a gestational carrier. So, you see all the sunsets here that seem dark but later, looking back, you marvel at how it all works out.

What if now, we find a surrogate, achieve our dreams and complete our family, and we somehow save me and my body any undue stress and more unexpected illness? Would that not be the most beautiful sunrise you have ever seen?

Life is full of ups and downs and there are no accidents. Take each day in stride and be more aware of your impact on others. Be kind to yourself. Spend time getting to know who you are and tune in to what feels good or bad. Follow your heart. Never have regrets and reach out to those in need. Get rid of jealousy and anger, and replace it with empathy and compassion. Thank your body for the work it does every day. If you can hear, cherish the sounds of the birds chirping. Put your smartphone down. Stay present and talk to your loved ones like you love them, and look into their eyes so they know you can hear them. I hope my book inspires you to live better than you ever thought possible, and that it helps open your eyes to the beauty that exists in every sunset.

# About the Author

Monique Williamson was born and raised on the Northshore of Vancouver, B.C. She has enjoyed a career in sales and marketing most of her life and also started the first successful Flying Wedge Pizza franchise in her early 20's. Most recently she enjoys success as a top producing real estate agent alongside her husband Jesse. Her life is kept busy caring for her 3 year old son Jack and 15 year old daughter Rachael. Monique intends on advocating on behalf of those who are too sick to do so , and eventually plans on speaking on the world stage speaking and sharing motivational and empowering messages she learned on her journey back to health.